ON BEING
FAMILY

A SOCIAL THEOLOGY
OF THE FAMILY

by
Ray S. Anderson
Dennis B. Guernsey

GRAND RAPIDS, MICHIGAN
WILLIAM B. EERDMANS PUBLISHING COMPANY

CONTENTS

72121

CONTENTS

PREFACE

E VERY human person is in some way connected to another person or persons. This is a necessary social reality, as well as a theological truth, for being connected means being human, and being human means being part of a family.

The connections that bind us to others are varied. Some are as thick as blood while others are as thin as a promise. There are bad connections that destroy the human spirit and there are good connections that create joy and hope.

In this book we will explore these connections in the context of the marvelous, complicated, and often contorted human family. Here we will set forth God's purpose in creating and preserving the human family as well as his goal for humans to create and experience their own life in family.

It is God's Word of creation that upholds the basic humanity of family, and it is God's work of covenant love that outlines the contours of family as the form of humanity that reflects his own image and likeness. We view the privilege of parenting and the pleasures of human love and sexuality as the social and spiritual realization of God's divine purpose for marriage and family. From the perspective of the church, as the new family of God, the human family is liberated from its own failures and fears, and each person is affirmed as having a place in God's kingdom. Through Jesus Christ, the brother to whom we are connected by grace, we are all brothers and sisters. We are family.

The authors, a family sociologist and a pastor/theologian, have combined many years of pastoral and counseling experience with research and reflection upon the formative and theoretical structures of family sociology and biblical theology. This book does not attempt to merge sociology with theology, nor does it attempt to synthesize social theory with biblical revelation into a single homogeneous presentation. Rather, each author, being committed to the authority of Scripture as normative, presents a chapter in each of the six major sections from his own particular perspective, either family sociology or theological anthropology. It is our hope that the readers will appreciate the two perspectives brought to each of the major units and will, by integrating them, develope their own theology of the family.

This material has been developed through several years of team teaching in the area of theology of the family. We wish to dedicate this book to the many students who have made their own contribution to it through their critical responses and creative application. We offer the book with the hope and prayer that it will contribute to the continued development of a theology of the family. It is our further hope that through this book many will discover new resources and new reasons to be hopeful about the family as a place where people can be connected to each other and to God "for good"!

Pasadena, California   RAY S. ANDERSON
August 1985   DENNIS B. GUERNSEY

Ray Anderson is Professor of Theology and Ministry at Fuller Theological Seminary. An ordained minister, he was the founding pastor of the Evangelical Free Church in Covina, California. Following eleven years of pastoral ministry, he studied at Edinburgh, Scotland, where he received his Ph.D. in theology.

Dennis Guernsey is Associate Professor of Marriage and Family Ministries and Director of the Institute for Marriage and Family Ministries at Fuller Theological Seminary. An ordained minister, he served on the staff of a large metropolitan church. In addition to his pastoral experience, he has served as the director of a community mental health agency and has 20 years experience as a marriage, family, and child counselor. He received his Ph.D. in Family Sociology from the University of Southern California and is an Approved Supervisor in the American Association of Marriage and Family Therapy.

PART ONE

CREATION AND THE FORMATION OF THE HUMAN FAMILY

CHAPTER ONE

A SOCIAL THEOLOGY
OF THE FAMILY

S EVERAL years ago, when Ray Anderson and I decided to team teach a course on the theology of the family, we began our preparations by making a thorough evaluation of the existing literature. We soon realized, however, that there was very little competent literature in the field of the theology of the family. There was, indeed, as a colleague has stated, a "massive gap" in this field — at least in terms of quality scholarship. Our search had uncovered less than a thousand pages of serious substantial Christian literature dealing with the area of the family from a rigorous theological perspective.

There are, however, hundreds — if not thousands — of popular volumes dealing with the family. Yet, as the following evaluation shows, this material seems in general to be deficient on at least three counts.

CONTEMPORARY APPROACHES
TO THE FAMILY

In the first place, most Christian literature dealing with the family at the popular level is *culturally encapsulated* — particularly Western and First World in its orientation. For example, missionary friends tell of a time when a famous Christian author, an expert in the area of marriage communication, visited their host country. As part of his presentation he asked the couples in the audience to draw their chairs together and face one another knee to knee and eye to eye. The white American missionaries in the audience did as they were told and were able to accomplish the task that was assigned them. The nationals who were in the audience were terribly uncomfortable and were unable to look their spouses in the eye, sitting knee to knee. Theirs was a culture in which public communication between husband and wife was seen as grossly inappropriate. In addition, they believed that to look anyone in the eye was to open oneself up to the influence of Satan.

After the meeting several of the missionaries suggested to the author that intimacy and communication could take alternate forms depending upon the culture. It didn't need to take place "knee to knee and eye to eye." However, the "expert" insisted that intimacy be defined his way because his way was "biblical." He was blinded by the influence of his own culture and naive as to the pervasiveness of culture itself.

How one believes things "ought to be" is usually influenced strongly by one's own cultural bias. As an institution, the family is the cradle of any culture. Thus, one's bias is established primarily through the influence of one's own family, which socializes its members into the specifics of its culture. This is particularly true with regard to the roles within the family, relationships and their nature, and the rules for those relationships.

Thus, probably in no area of study and discussion will matters of culture be more intrusive than in those having to do with the family. In my opinion, most popular literature about the family, including that which I myself have written, naively sets forth cultural specifics as if they were biblical absolutes.

Unfortunately, this limits the meaning and influence of these materials when they are used cross-culturally. Just at a time when the family as an institution is experiencing stress and pressure multiculturally, we render ineffective the solutions needed to cope with this stress. Subsequently, we silence the dialog needed to bring the truth of Scripture to bear upon the issues.

To rectify this situation, we need responsible scholars to enter into a cross-cultural reflection on matters having to do with the family. (This is being done in almost every other area of significance to the church, i.e., in the translation of Scripture and in evangelism.) Until this happens, the supposed "answers" we bring should be couched in the subjunctive rather than the indicative. Until then, we should admit to our audiences that there are as many questions as there are answers in our teaching. It is not wrong to admit that we are culturally encapsulated. It is, in fact, the beginning of the process of being set free.

Second, contemporary Christian approaches to the study of the family are *naively influenced by psychology.*[1] In one sense, this falls under the category of cultural encapsulation. However, I think it needs to be highlighted because of its significance. The discipline of psychology has established as its agenda the understanding and the growth of the individual as a person.[2] It has, as much as has any other discipline, addressed itself to matters related to the family. However, psychology has struggled with understanding the family itself as a unit. The disparity between the views of the person as an individual

---

1. I am indebted to my colleague Jack Balswick for his insights in this matter. They have been set forth in his unpublished manuscript, "The Psychological Captivity of Evangelicalism," Fuller Theological Seminary, n.d.

2. See A. H. Maslow, "A Theory of Human Motivation," *Psychological Review* 50 (1943): 370-96, for an old but significant statement of the psychological task.

and the person as a member of a family has created a difficult if not irreconcilable tension for some within the discipline.[3]

Disciplines such as sociology and social work, on the other hand, have contributed significantly to the field. It would seem that their openness to the idea and nature of systems has contributed to their acceptance of the person as part of a family.

But when it comes to the study of the family from a Christian point of view, most contributors are either practicing psychologists, such as James Dobson and Bruce Narramore, or they have been primarily influenced by psychology, as seems to be the case with Norman Wright and Jay Adams. As a result of this influence, their works tend to display the form of psychology that is determinative for each: behaviorism for Dobson, psychoanalysis for Narramore, and reality therapy for both Wright and Adams.[4]

However, what is at issue here is not the influence of psychology in the writings of Christian authors but our failure to admit to that influence and to acknowledge its significance. The difficulty comes when truth claims are made and the teaching of a psychological issue is made coequal with the teaching of Scripture. Unfortunately, the Christian public is unable to tell the difference. The responsibility for distinguishing between the two lies not with the reading public but with the authors and their interpreters.

Therefore, the authors of this present volume acknowledge the influence and deliberate use of the disciplines of sociology and General Systems Theory as well as social psychology. The emphasis here is upon the word *social*. We have intentionally used those disciplines that seem to us to have the most to say about the person in his or her social contexts. We believe the family as an institution is best understood as a relational or social phenomenon. In fact, we would go so far as to say that psychology as a discipline has had an inordinate influence upon Christian literature about the family and that that influence has yielded an untowardly narrow view of the issues. This book is our attempt to approach the task from a different and, we hope, more profitable perspective.

The third criticism of contemporary Christian approaches to the family is that they are too often *biblically superficial and theologically shallow*. It seems that Christian publishers and authors have responded to the cries of the Christian public for help in this area and not to an imperative from within

---

3. The works of Carl Whitaker chronicle this tension. See *From Psyche to System: The Evolving Therapy of Carl Whitaker*, ed. John R. Neill and David P. Kniskern (New York: The Guilford Press, 1982).

4. See James Dobson, *Dare to Discipline* (Glendale, CA: Regal Books, 1974); Bruce Narramore, *Help! I'm a Parent* (Grand Rapids: Zondervan, 1972); H. Norman Wright, *Marriage Counseling* (San Francisco: Harper and Row, 1982); Jay Adams, *Competent to Counsel* (Nutley, NJ: Presbyterian and Reformed, 1972).

Scripture itself. This cry for help from the Christian public, which legitimately established the agenda, was answered first by Christian helping-professionals. Unfortunately, biblical and theological scholars have been slow to respond. Yet the Christian public equates much of what has been written as thoroughly biblical and appropriately theological. They do so because there are very few models of solid biblical exegesis and theological reflection to guide them. Psychology stepped in when theology failed to act.

To solve this dilemma, respected biblical and theological scholars need to develop appropriate models for the church's use rather than abandon the field to secular disciplines. Someone must take up the challenge. Those of us in the helping professions cannot be faulted because what we do, we do naively. The burden now shifts to those who claim to be experts in the fields of Scripture and theology. Whether or not they pick up that gauntlet remains to be seen.

WHAT IS A SOCIAL THEOLOGY OF THE FAMILY?

As we have said, a more useful and ultimately more productive course is to explore the models suggested by the social sciences rather than the philosophical models, which dominate both traditional and contemporary theology, or the individualistic psychological models, which dominate contemporary popular Christian literature.

According to Gregory Baum, theology has been unduly influenced for the most part by the discipline of philosophy. By its very nature theology is an eclectic discipline and, as such, easily becomes dependent upon alien explanations of reality without thinking through the implications of those explanations. In the past, theology has relied upon the disciplines of history and literary analysis as means for unlocking the meaning of Scripture and has used philosophy for setting forth theological models for the organization of that meaning. Baum suggests that a more profitable use can and should be made of other models.[5]

The family has always been a social institution. When it comes to the study of the family and the creation of models by which the family can be understood, we believe that the social sciences provide appropriate and beneficial tools for the understanding of the family as an institution and, hence, an understanding of what the Bible tells us about the family.

What we are suggesting, therefore, is that the burgeoning area of secular material about the family as it is perceived as a social institution might be a

---

5. See Gregory Baum, *Religion and Alienation* (New York: Paulist Press, 1975).

useful field in which to explore the meaning of Scripture. With this in mind, we offer our model of a social theology of the family.

As a means of setting forth our model, we will begin with a discussion of the major orientations that define the boundaries of our methodology and then we will set forth the four major assumptions that underlie our model.

METHODOLOGY OF A SOCIAL THEOLOGY OF THE FAMILY

Our methodology suggests two major orientations, each of which has a specific contribution and a social focus.

The first dimension of our methodology is its *systems orientation*. This can best be explained by an example from the sphere of science. One of the most significant achievements in the twentieth century has been the solving of the riddle as to how information is transmitted through the genetic process. As geneticists dealt with the problem of heredity, they were faced with the question of how so much data could be transmitted through so few genes. The detailed structure of the adult individual was far too complicated for the data to be stored directly in the genes. If, as they originally supposed, the process was linear and there was a direct causal relationship between the first cell and the characteristics of the fully developed and mature individual, then the problem was immense.

The solution lay not in the discovery of a complicated direct causal relationship but in the discovery that genes carry a set of rules to generate the interrelationships between the genes. The key to understanding this was a shift from thinking in terms of the direct causal structure between properties to recognizing the generation of rules that govern the relationship between properties. That shift in emphasis was provoked by the influence of modern systems theory.

What do we mean when we use the term *system?* Ivan Steiner defines it as a "cluster of highly interrelated parts, each responding to the others, the entire set somehow maintaining itself as a distinguishable whole in spite of incessant internal change."[6] The emphasis of the definition is upon the idea that the whole is something more than the sum of the parts. The question is, what is that "something more"?

According to Sir Arthur Eddington, a famous British scientist, "We often think that when we have completed our study of one we know all about two,

6. See Ivan Steiner, *Group Processes and Productivity* (New York: Academic Press, 1972).

because 'two is one and one.' We forget that we still have to make a study of 'and.' . . . The study of 'and' [is the] study of organization."[7]

The concept of "system," then, has to do with elevating the importance of relationship, even recognizing the priority of relationship in the understanding of complex mechanical, physical, and social systems. The application of the concept to the fields of modern science has yielded an understanding of the plan, method, order, and arrangement between the entities or properties those sciences attempt to study and describe. As was the case of the geneticists who unlocked the mysteries of the double helix, modern science now focuses upon the nature and understanding of the whole as being something more than the sum of the parts. Science and system have become inextricably linked.

The body of literature that has come to describe this process and the theoretical model used therein is called General Systems Theory. General Systems Theory is concerned with developing a systematic theoretical framework for describing relationships in the empirical world. Theorists such as von Bertallanffy and Boulding suggest that the order that lies beneath all sciences can, in fact, be described. General Systems Theory is one attempt to do so.[8]

In the same way that General Systems Theory has provoked radical insights into such dissimilar fields as biology and physics, it likewise provides a rich source of material in the construction of a theology of the family. What was useful in unraveling the mysteries of DNA and the double helix might also be useful in unraveling some of the hermeneutical and theological problems that plague the serious student of Scripture as he or she attempts to solve the puzzle of the relationship between New Testament teaching about family and the relevance of that teaching for today. Therefore, when we refer to a "social theology of the family" we are referring to a systems orientation.

The second major orientation of our social theology of the family is its *ecological orientation*. Urie Bronfenbrenner has likened the ecological environment to a set of nested structures, each inside the next.[9] The innermost level, the microsystem, is the immediate setting of the human person. This can be the home, the school, the church, and so forth.

The next level is the mesosystem, or the interrelationship between two or more settings in which the person actively participates. For example, a child may be involved simultaneously in the home, the school, and the peer group.

---

7. See Sir Arthur Eddington, *The Nature of the Physical World* (Ann Arbor: University of Michigan Press, 1958).

8. See L. von Bertalanffy, *General Systems Theory* (New York: George Braziller, 1968); Kenneth Boulding, "General Systems Theory — The Skeleton of Science," in L. von Bertalanffy, ed., *General Systems* 1 (1956).

9. See Urie Bronfenbrenner, *The Ecology of Human Development* (Cambridge: Harvard University Press, 1979).

The conditions that constitute the relationships between these interlocking systems form the boundaries of the mesosystem.

The third level is that of the exosystem, one or more settings that do not involve the person as an active participant, but in which events occur that affect, or are affected by, what happens in the setting containing the developing person. Thus a parent's workplace is part of the child's exosystem because what transpires there can dramatically alter the child's world—for example, when the parent is unemployed or relocated due to occupational migration.

The fourth and final level is that of the macrosystem. Bronfenbrenner defines this level as consisting of lower order systems (micro-, meso-, and exo-) that exist, or could exist, at the level of the subculture or the culture as a whole, along with any belief systems or ideology underlying such systems. It is the belief and ideational environment of which the person is a part. Its boundaries are diffuse but highly significant.

In terms of a social theology of the family, an ecological orientation involves the complex, interlocking relationships between the four system levels and demands that they be taken into account in the construction of the perceptual world of the family. Thus, the person cannot be isolated and defined only at the microsystem level. He or she is much more—and the "much more" is the stuff of which a social theology of the family is made.

Having suggested the two major orientations that make up the methodology of our social theology of the family, the system and the ecological, we turn now to a discussion of the assumptions that undergird this methodology.

ASSUMPTIONS OF A SOCIAL THEOLOGY OF THE FAMILY

In the first place, a social theology of the family is *deliberately non-Cartesian rather than Cartesian* in its explanation of reality. Again, an example from the field of the sciences will illustrate this point.

In *The Turning Point*, Fritjof Capra traces the influence of General Systems Theory upon the hard sciences.[10] Beginning with the discipline of physics, he follows the failure of Newtonian explanations of reality and the success of what he calls "the New Physics" and its ability to define the nature of quantum mechanics. In order to explain phenomenon at the subatomic level, scientists in the field of quantum physics had to abandon their previously held reductionistic explanations of reality. Since Newton, the task of science had been to follow Descartes and to reduce the world to its progressively smaller and more "accurate" properties—the Cartesian approach. When the scientists

---

10. See Fritjof Capra, *The Turning Point* (New York: Bantam Books, 1983).

studying quantum mechanics began to understand the nature of the reality they were observing, however, they found that they had moved from reductionistic explanations toward those that defined the subatomic world in terms of relationships rather than in terms of things. The old rules no longer were adequate for the task. The handmaiden of their new search was a systems explanation of what they were perceiving. In order to understand reality at that level they had to throw away their previously held Cartesian assumptions. The result, according to Capra, was a conceptual revolution.

Capra goes on to suggest that this new non-Cartesian approach has been useful as well in the areas of biomedical research, psychology, and economics. The difficulty lies, he states, in the fact that old Newtonian models persist even when they prove to be outmoded and unhelpful.

For example, Newtonian explanations of psychological reality inevitably lead to the reductionistic observations and understanding of the individual. Hence, we see the dominance of Newtonian thought in contemporary psychological research and explanation. In other words, "Cartesian" explanations of the family ultimately lead us to descriptions and explanations of the individuals who make up that family — not to an understanding of the dynamics of relationships within the family and between its members. The Cartesian path always leads the observer to reduce the family to its supposedly smallest parts.

A "non-Cartesian" approach, on the other hand, suggests that individuals do not, in fact, exist. Said radically, human persons ultimately are only members to be understood in the context of their social systems. Similarly, such an approach suggests that human persons can be understood only as persons-in-relationship.[11]

The second assumption of our social theology of the family is that it is *systemic rather than linear* in its understanding of causality. Traditionally, thinking about the family (and other essentially hierarchical social systems) has been based on a Newtonian assumption of linear cause and effect relationships. The patterns of cause and effect are strung together like a row of dominos — they tend to be one-directional rather than multidirectional. For example, the cause of an adolescent's poor self-esteem might be seen to be a poor relationship with his or her parent(s), and the cause of that difficulty might be their similarly low self-esteem. The child or the adolescent is always an effect and the parents are always a cause. If a wife is experiencing difficulty, a Newtonian linear, reductionistic explanation assumes that the cause is always the husband. Such "chain of command" thinking is necessarily linear.

A more systemic model assumes that what is on the one hand effect can

11. See Ray S. Anderson, *On Being Human* (Grand Rapids: Eerdmans, 1982), for a more detailed explanation of this phenomenon.

through the process of feedback also function as cause. In such a case, the adolescent can as much cause the parents' low self-esteem as the parents can cause the adolescent's. Wives can be as responsible for marital dysfunction as can husbands. Human persons in relationship can be thought of — and, in fact, should be thought of — as both cause and effect simultaneously.

Thus, a systemic rather than a linear assumption leads to an emphasis upon the patterns of relationship between and among the members of a system instead of an emphasis upon identifying an ultimate cause.

Our third assumption flows naturally out of the first two and is stated for purposes of emphasis. It is that a social theology of the family is *relationalistic rather than reductionistic*. By this we mean that the human person must ultimately be held accountable for what H. Richard Niebuhr refers to as that person's "fitting" behavior. The "responsible self" is the person who accepts his or her membership in a community (or social system) in such a way as to contribute to the benefit and health of that community.[12]

"You shall love the Lord your God," "You shall love your neighbor" and "You shall love yourself" are systemically and inextricably linked. If you interpret these three commands linearly, as if one is cause and the other(s) effect, the teaching becomes weighted in one direction as opposed to another. The first commandment, "You shall love the Lord your God," becomes an integral part of the second and third only if it is linked with them systemically. Thus, loving God, loving your neighbor, and loving yourself are understood best of all in the context of our relationalistic assumption.

The fourth assumption that underlies our thinking is that a social theology of the family is fundamentally *dynamic rather than static*. By *dynamic* we mean that emphasis is placed upon process rather than structure (although structure is admittedly important). The greater difficulty in understanding a family is to understand how it adapts and changes in the midst of a complex environment while at the same time it maintains its stability. (This process will be discussed in detail in Chapter Four.) Our non-Cartesian, systemic, and relationalistic assumptions coalesce to place the emphasis upon adaptation rather than function, upon flexibility rather than rigidity.

In sum, we must define the family as an institution — as a creative, pulsing, changing, adapting system capable of survival. Thus, we interpret words of doom and despair about the threatened existence of the family as the attempt of a broader system to preserve the past rather than find ways of adapting to the future. The family itself is not under attack — only one form of the family is. Only the encapsulated perceptions of a Western, technological mind-set

---

12. See H. Richard Niebuhr, *The Responsible Self* (New York: Harper and Row, 1963).

insist that the family be defined as the nuclear, Mom-Dad-and-the-Kids institution. Perhaps it is that narrow definition of family that is under attack. Our emphasis upon process allows us to envision the future of the family with hope rather than with despair.

HOW DOES A SOCIAL THEOLOGY OF THE FAMILY APPROACH THE THEOLOGICAL TASK?

In the next chapter Ray Anderson suggests that our theological task is "to probe the depths and dimensions of a divinely created system of human existence in community called family, and to set forth the intrinsic order of this social system as grounded in the revealed purpose and will of God." The key concept is the idea of intrinsic order. Traditionally we have interpreted that order as an organizational chart, with its positions defined by God in Scripture. In contrast, we are suggesting another way of looking at the issue: a flow chart that captures the nature of the relationships between the members of the system rather than emphasizes their position. By focusing upon the nature of relationships we are able to maintain the integrity of Scripture and its influence upon the family while at the same time leave room for the family's adaptation and creative response to its environment.

A second consideration in our approach to the theological task has to do with our praxis orientation.[13] Because we focus upon the nature of social relationships, it naturally follows that we focus upon ministry as well. In fact, we view the task of theology and the task of ministry to be systemically related. Good theology works. Bad theology doesn't. Said in another way, God's revelation of himself to humanity inevitably leads to imperatives of action. You cannot have faith without works. The theological task begins with members of the system asking themselves what are the implications of our theology for each ecological level and ends with a commitment to action as to what must be done accordingly. The primary task, therefore, of a social theology of the family is its ultimate action orientation. "What shall we then do?" becomes the imperative and the tension we must all live with. If it works, it requires us all to count the cost and to choose this day whom we shall serve.

---

13. See Robin Gill, "From Sociology to Theology," in *Sociology and Theology,* ed. David Martin, John Orme Mills, and W. S. F. Pickering (New York: St. Martin's Press, 1980).

CHAPTER TWO

THE OLD COMMANDMENT
WHICH IS ALSO
A NEW COMMANDMENT

T HE story has it that as Adam and Eve were being escorted out of the Garden of Eden, having disobeyed God and suffered the consequences, Adam turned to Eve and said, "My dear, we are living in a changing world!"

Indeed, the more things change, the more they stay the same, according to the French proverb. This is certainly true with respect to family life, which continues to undergo radical and often precipitous change, in what is now the last quarter of the twentieth century.[1] But is this in itself sufficient cause to warrant yet another book on the subject? When a pastor/theologian and a family sociologist combine to write a book on the family, one would have good reason to suspect that there is an agenda hidden beneath the somewhat trendy appearance of a book that picks up on a contemporary theme and speaks to modern anxieties.

Yes, there is an agenda. The Judeo-Christian tradition has lived so long with its implicit assumptions concerning the fundamental value and structure of family that is has often forgotten to make these assumptions explicit. More specifically, from within the Christian church, and particularly from the perspective of evangelical Christian faith and experience, our agenda is to clarify and make explicit theological assumptions concerning the family as a basic social structure. We are not simply reacting against modernity and change in an attempt to justify a conservatism that only looks back with longing for the "good old days." Rather, our agenda is to probe the depths and dimensions of a divinely created system of human existence in community called family, and

---

1. Brigitte and Peter Berger, in their book, *The War Over the Family* (Garden City, NY: Doubleday, Anchor Press, 1983), offer a brief but helpful discussion of the evolution of the "problem of the family," particularly from the time of the Enlightenment to the present. Despite modernity, the Bergers argue, the family structure has not changed as much as many contemporary analysts have charged (pp. 91-92). The basic thesis of the book is that the "bourgeois family," or "middle-class family," with its structure of clearly defined roles for mother, father, and child, is not a dispensable structure but, rather, continues to be the best alternative, all things considered, in the face of modern challenges to family structures and roles (p. 167).

to set forth the intrinsic order of this social system as grounded in the revealed purpose and will of God.

In this chapter I want to raise questions from a critical and theological perspective concerning the nature of that intrinsic order of the family system. Following that, I will attempt to draw forth certain implications of a biblical doctrine of creation as it pertains to the formation of the family as an essential structure of human society. My specific goal will be to show how the essential structure of family can be open to change and adaptation in its social environment without losing its character as a created and divinely determined order of human existence.

IS THERE A QUINTESSENTIAL STRUCTURE OF THE FAMILY?

The ancient Greeks recognized four basic elements as essential to the structure of the physical world: fire, air, water, and earth. The fifth and highest essence — the quintessence — was that substance upon which the structure of the observable world was built: the element that permeated all of nature. The family, as one of the oldest structures of human society — if not the oldest — has several elements, as any textbook on family sociology or cultural anthropology will tell us. But is there a quintessence of the family, an original or underlying structure upon which all of the other elements rest?

If there is, we cannot find it by studying the origin of the family in the human race. According to Professor Bernard I. Murstein, "the truth of the matter is that we do not know with even a modest degree of certitude how the family actually got started."[2] The current literature in sociology of the family cannot give us a definitive conclusion as to how the family originated as a social structure. In the biblical literature, on the other hand, the brief creation account concludes with the laconic statement, "Therefore a man leaves his father and his mother and cleaves to his wife, and they become one flesh" (Gen. 2:24). While this might be construed as a cryptic statement of what the quintessence of marriage is, it only presupposes that the readers already know what a family is — that relationship between parents and children that is left behind for the creation of a new relationship.

Of course, we must remember that the creation account was written in the context of a people who had experienced the great event of covenant making firsthand, which was accomplished through an exodus from captivity and entrance into a land of promise. This covenant of liberation and promise, however, was anchored in the covenant God had already made with Abraham

---

2. Bernard I. Murstein, *Love, Sex and Marriage Through the Ages* (New York: Springer, 1974), p. 14.

when he promised that "I will bless those who bless you, and him who curses you I will curse; and by you all the families of the earth will bless themselves" (Gen. 12:3).

Much later in that same tradition, the apostle Paul wrote, "I bow my knees before the Father, from whom every family in heaven and on earth is named" (Eph. 3:14-15). This doxological statement suggests that there is a quintessential order of the family, and that God himself is the quintessence. But this will not have much meaning for us unless we examine it more critically from the perspective of how the social structure of a family might be related to an essential element or cause. For the purpose of our discussion, we will construct a somewhat simplistic typology to elucidate the matter more clearly.

In the first place, one could account for the existence of the family through some form of *natural or biological determinism*. That is, the family has an intrinsic order that is determined by a natural or biological order. Stephen Clark, for example, follows the traditional approach in Roman Catholic theology by holding that the created and biological nature of human persons is determinative for the order of grace. Thus, he argues that male and female sexual differentiation is "created into the human race." He further argues that the intrinsic order of male and female in the marriage relation as well as within the family structure is determined by nature and biology, and is thus not susceptible to change by any form of grace.[3]

From this it follows that the social form of the family is under the determinism of the natural or biological form of human existence. While sin enters in so as to create disorder, the fundamental natural order of the family is not destroyed. Furthermore, the renewed humanity offered through Jesus Christ does not establish a new order of family. Even the church as the community of Christ must be structured in such a way, Clark argues, that it upholds the natural order of the family rather than constitutes a new order of family.

Obviously, this natural or biological determinism occurs in a variety of forms, but they all have in common the principles of causality and necessity. Any change in the form is a violation of the original cause, and is viewed as disorder and confusion. When Mary's friends at church tell her that by leaving her children with a babysitter so she can pursue a career she is disobeying

---

3. Stephen Clark, *Man and Woman in Christ* (Ann Arbor: Servant Books, 1980), pp. 440-41, 447, 448. The seeds of this concept of a natural order for role relationships between men and women are sown deep in the Reformers as well. Luther, commenting on the relation between men and women in the marriage role said, "This distinction is made in nature and in God's creation also, where no woman (still less children and fools) can or ought to exercise rule, as experience tells us, and as Moses says, "Thou shalt be in subjection to thy husband' (Gen. 3:16). The gospel does not abolish this natural law, but confirms it as the ordinance and creation of God." *The Works of Martin Luther*, ed. Henry Eyster Jacobs (Philadelphia: Muhlenberg Press, 1915-43), 5:276.

God, she should not expect them to give her a proof text from the Bible to support the admonition. Rather, the implication is that God's will for her, as part of the intrinsic natural order, is to be in subordination to her husband and in the role of nurturer rather than provider.

A second way of accounting for the existence of the family in any given cultural context is in the form of a *natural or cultural indeterminism*. In other words, the form of any particular expression of personal or social relationship is not determined by any intrinsic order or contingent on a law of necessary forms. As Ross Bender puts it,

> Many different illustrations of the new social order that is being advocated share one underlying assumption, that the fulfillment and the self-realization of the individual are the measure of all things. If the individual's well-being is enhanced by any given relationship or social grouping, well and good. If it is frustrated by one's commitment to another, that commitment may be, indeed must be, withdrawn.[4]

In this view, neither natural law nor cultural precedent can be allowed to determine the freedom of the human person to form relationships that are mutually fulfilling. And the converse is also held to be true. That which is mutually satisfying and which takes place between "consenting adults," so the logic goes, cannot violate any law of God or of nature.

Further, some contemporary theologians believe that this view of natural or cultural indeterminism is not opposed to Christian theology. They argue on behalf of a complete freedom for men and women to establish the character of social roles in marriage and family. Professor Letty Russell, for example, rejects the creation account as a starting point for establishing the meaning of contemporary roles and relationships between men and women. Instead, she begins with the new creation in Christ, not with the original creation mandate, and holds that mutuality and partnership is itself a creative order characterized by sharing, giving, and receiving.[5]

Perhaps we can see this perspective as a reaction against the determinism of a natural or biological order, with a more hopeful emphasis upon the freedom of the personal and individual sphere of human existence as the quintessence of the social sphere. This view is supported theologically by those who hold to the radical judgment of the new order of being through Christ, over against the old order. That is, proponents of this view say that social relationships that are marked by traditional roles, rooted in nature and culture, are part of that which is "passing away," while that which the Word of God upholds through grace is new and liberating. Thus, when John is told by his

---

4. Ross Bender, *Christians in Families* (Scottdale, PA: Herald Press, 1982), p. 42.
5. Letty Russell, *The Future of Partnership* (Philadelphia: Westminster Press, 1979), pp. 49-53.

Christian friends that he is living under bondage to the law and not under grace because he continues to be faithful in a marriage that has become a burden and practically devoid of intimacy, he should not expect them to accept his appeal to the biblical teaching concerning the indissolubility of marriage.

Obviously, these two representatives of a typology for elucidating perspectives on the family are stylized and artificial. However, they do serve well to show the opposite tendencies of determinism and indeterminism with respect to natural order and the social structure of the family. We have set forth these two perspectives in order to make more clear the contours of a third perspective within this typology, by which we seek to escape the dilemma of determinism on the one hand, and indeterminism on the other.

We will call this third perspective a *natural or created contingent order*. That which is contingent is an event that may or may not occur with regard to natural laws — thus, it is not necessary when viewed from the principle of causality. If an event *is* contingent with regard to natural laws, it is dependent upon something outside of its own structure of being, even though it has its own order and structure.

For example, we can view the natural world as contingent upon a source beyond its own structures and laws. When applied to the natural world, a contingent order is a created order; that is, it exists in such a way that its own natural order is established by a higher order. The higher order is absolute, while the natural order is relative to the higher order, even in its apparent stability. Thus, the natural world is created by and contingent upon the Creator for its original and continued existence. "Heaven and earth will pass away, but my words will not pass away," said Jesus (Luke 21:33).

It seems, therefore, that there *is* a quintessential order for the family as a social structure. However, the quintessence is not located within the natural order as the determinist would have it, nor in the freedom of the individual to create a social structure, as the indeterminist would have it. The quintessence of the social structure we call family is rooted in the creative Word of God and its purpose, which expresses itself through the order of creation. The creative Word gives form and stability to the natural order as the context for the formation of the human family. Yet the form of the family as a social structure is always contingent upon that essential order which belongs to God as the Creator and which constitutes the absolute order to which all else is relative.

Theological anthropology, drawing upon biblical teaching, makes a similar conclusion with regard to the form and structure of humanity itself. The solitary person cannot share fully in the complete human existence when it is seen as a social relation. According to the creation account in Genesis 2, cohumanity is the original and, therefore, the quintessential aspect of personal and individual human existence. But this basic social structure is itself contingent upon the reality of God as a personal order of being, with human existence created in his likeness and image.[6]

If we choose the third perspective in our typology as more authentically biblical, certain advantages immediately become apparent. First, we can see that the natural and social order of human existence is essential to the formation of the human family; furthermore, there is a fundamental continuity of order from the beginning of the human family up to and through the present age. At the same time, we can recognize that the natural order is not itself absolutely determinative for the social order of the family. It is essential but not quintessential, in the sense that we have developed the concept. In the same way that the Israelites understood Yahweh to have named himself with regard to their existence as a people of God, that is, as the "I AM WHO I AM," or, better, "I AM HE WHO WILL BE THERE FOR YOU" (Exod. 3:14), we can understand that God continues to be the formative presence and power for the social structure of his people.[7] The I AM entails the authority that gives form to the original creation, but it also entails the authority to uphold the continuity of creation through the changing of form.

Here, then, is the way in which we can begin to understand the continuity of structure as a social reality through the changing of social forms and even social roles. For Jesus, the I AM continues to be the authority for preserving the old (I have not come to destroy the law; Matt. 5:17), but also for mandating the new ("What God has cleansed you must not call common"; Acts 10:15).

Because love is a quintessential structure of relationship, rooted in God's own being, the structure of social relationships remains normative even though the roles through which that structure is expressed change. In the Old Testament, the commandment of love that connected Israel as a contingent social order to God through the covenant required the observance of specific role functions and regulations, including a patriarchal family structure. In the New Testament, the same commandment of love is expressed as a form of normative social relationship that makes these regulations and roles relative to a new form of family life and structure. Here we see that God's anointing through the Holy Spirit comes upon men and women indiscriminately (Acts 1:14; 2:1-4). The older structure of social forms of community and the family continues, as could be expected, but God's purpose in the formation of the

---

6. For a more complete exposition of the concept of contingent order in theological anthropology, see Ray S. Anderson, *On Being Human* (Grand Rapids: Eerdmans, 1982), chaps. 1-2. For a theological study of the concept of contingent order, see Thomas F. Torrance, *Divine and Contingent Order* (Oxford: Oxford University Press, 1981).

7. For a recent discussion of the biblical concept of the name of God as I AM WHO I AM, see George A. F. Knight, *I AM: This is My Name* (Grand Rapids: Eerdmans, 1983).

human family now becomes increasingly clear—the structure of love is to be expressed in new forms of social and family life.

The apostle John, toward the end of that first century, put quite simply what we have been saying:

> Beloved, I am writing you no new commandment, but an old commandment which you had from the beginning; the old commandment is the word which you have heard. Yet I am writing you a new commandment, which is true in him and in you, because the darkness is passing away and the true light is already shining. (1 John 2:7-8)

The new commandment which is also old is, of course, the commandment of love.

We must now delineate the implications of the creative commandment of love as a structure of social relationships through which God gives the original and continuing form of the human family. This we will do by looking more closely at the concept of order as contingent, creative, and conventional.

CONTINGENT ORDER AND THE STABILITY OF THE SOCIAL STRUCTURE

One of the basic problems that plagues any attempt to speak of authority and stability in the process of change is that of the relation of the absolute to that which is relative. The traditionalist tends to absolutize the form of the old and to relativize the form of the new. If it is old it is true, the adage goes, and if it is new it is false! The ancient Greeks solved this problem by absolutizing the form, or idea, of a thing, setting it apart from the phenomenon, or appearance of a thing. Thus, they could have stability and order while at the same time allow for the semblance of change; all at the expense, of course, of the reality of the physical and temporal structure of the world.

In biblical theology, God himself is the absolute and, therefore, quintessential reality that upholds all created reality. However, this is not the same as the "final cause" of the medieval philosophers, who argued from effect back to cause. Rather, God is the creative power and reality that participates in and upholds the very structures of the world—including the social structure of the human family. It is in this sense that we have said that the social structure of the human family is a contingent order—a true order of social relationships, which embodies the purpose of the Creator. Yet God, the Lord and Creator, remains the absolute order and power that upholds the relative order and power of the created world. We can account for what appear to be invariable laws of nature by the fact that the created order is a true order, set within the bounds of God's determinative will and purpose. This gives stability to the created order without simultaneously investing it with laws that are absolutely determinative of its own nature and destiny.

In other words (altering the concept of the ancient Greeks to bring it more in line with a biblical view of reality), no created structure of reality contains within it its own telos, or ultimate goal. There are, to be sure, limited forms of purpose and goal within the natural world, but the telos, which gives meaning to the created process, resides in the Word of God. However, this absolute purpose, or telos, which gives created and contingent reality its true order, is also embodied within the structures of created reality — such as the family.

Thus, we do not look for the origin of the family in some primitive instincts of barely human creatures, but rather we find it disclosed to us in the revealed purpose for the most basic human relationship: "Therefore ... they become one flesh" (Gen. 2:24). The fundamental structures of human social relationships embody the divine purpose that human persons should reflect the image and likeness of God. Cultural anthropologists discuss the primitive needs of emerging domesticity, economic survival, and erotic sexual fulfillment to account for the formation of the family as a social unit. But these needs and instincts will always be ambiguous and fraught with failure. The stability of the family is rooted in God's purpose, which is expressed through the relative and fallible forms of social order. After all, the command of God, which reached back into the creation account to establish the true order and purpose of the human family, came in the context of a highly patriarchical society.

God's command, therefore, is expressed in quite specific commands and regulations for the establishment of the social order of the family. To the extent that these commands and regulations conform to the divine purpose and assist in upholding the intrinsic structure of relationships as grounded in love, they are carried along with the community of those who live under the command of God. But when the commandments become detached from this quintessential purpose and are made into a law that claims absolute power in its own right, the commandment becomes an absolute form of the command of God. This is no doubt what happened in the case of the commandment concerning the sabbath.

The command to honor the sabbath day was originally given to uphold the core social structure of the covenant community as contingent upon the power and love of God, not upon natural determinism. The religious legalists, however, absolutized the command into a law that stood in judgment of God himself. Jesus, however, made the commandment relative to God's command when he said, "The Son of man is lord of the sabbath" (Luke 6:5), further teaching that "The sabbath was made for man, not man for the sabbath" (Mark 2:27). By no means could this be construed as negating the sabbath itself as the embodiment of the command of God. The intrinsic structure of peace (*shalom*) and rest, which belongs to God alone and which he shares with his own creatures as a gift, is upheld as quintessential to human life.

In the same way, then, we can now see that social regulations are related to an intrinsic, core structure of social reality and are effective to the extent that they serve to uphold that core reality. Even circumcision became dispensable when the core reality of a "circumcision of the heart" came to be experienced through the gift of the Holy Spirit. Circumcision, as a sign of the covenant relation and of the obedience that this relation entailed, could give way to other signs that upheld the same core relation between God and his people.

In other words, in a contingent order of basic social relationships as created by God, relation serves as the logic of rules. And the core structure of relation is itself contingent upon and upheld by God's absolute order of being. This is what gives stability and continuity to the formation of family as a social order within the created order. But this too needs further elaboration.

CREATIVE ORDER
AND THE FORMATION
OF THE FAMILY STRUCTURE

It is important for us to remember that the original order that constitutes the integrity of the social unit called the family is not merely the result of the first and most primitive attempts to develop family out of ambiguous needs and motives. Nor is the original order an ideal that never quite can be identified with the social order for the sake of protecting its infallibility and perfection. The ancient Greeks, especially Plato, thought this was their only option. In their thought, order itself must be absolute and thereby perfect. In biblical theology, on the other hand, one never grants to order as a social structure of reality the perfection and absolute quality that is reserved for God alone.

The creative order is, as we have said, God's purpose embodied in a concrete social order, which is itself culturally relative. Thus, certain aspects of the ancient Semitic culture became part of the divine order embodied in the structure of the covenant. It is well known that circumcision was not a ritual limited to the descendants of Abraham, but as a cultural practice it became part of the covenant promise, thereby becoming a sign of the creative, covenant order of Israel. When circumcision was no longer an essential sign of God's own purpose, it could be dispensed with as a sign of the covenant.

This principle is difficult to grasp, particularly within the structure of biblical revelation. That which is culturally relative becomes the embodiment of the absolute command of God without becoming itself an absolute element in that order. According to the Israelites, the person who disobeyed the commandment concerning circumcision was opposed to God and defied his purpose. However, there came a time when to insist on the necessity of circumcision for entrance into the kingdom of God (as a cause-and-effect relationship) was itself viewed as opposition to God. This is a moment of truth that escaped the apostle Peter but was crystal clear to Paul, as witnessed by his rebuke of Peter at Antioch (cf. Gal. 2:11-21). But it would be wrong to conclude from this relative aspect of a rule or commandment that the formation of the social relation called the family is indeterminate. If we do, we fail to understand the nature of the biblical concept of contingence and the creative command of God.

The authority of the creative Word of God never passes on to the form of its embodiment, which would result in a new principle of causality. Rather, there is a continuity of order throughout the process of the formation of the family. By "principle of causality" we mean a relation established between form and content with regard to the command of God such that it can be absolutely determined that one who practices the form is also a participant in the resulting divine order of the Word. What must be made clear here is the biblical distinction between "form" in the sense of a rigid or nonchanging structure, and "form" as a dynamic and intrinsically structured reality and order, which entails what we have called "formation." The human family is thus a formation of God's purpose with its own intrinsic structure of relationships, which we could call "rules" or "laws" of relationship. These cannot be deduced out of the structures of natural law, but neither can they be left to individuals to create as a means of satisfying their own needs or desires.

As we have already noted, the actual structure of this "inner logic" of social relation unique to the formation of the family is grounded in the intentionality and practice of love. Thus, the apostle Paul writes the headline over his practical instructions for the family: "walk in love, as Christ loved us" (Eph. 5:1). Paul then discusses what it means to exemplify this quintessential element in a variety of relationships, from the broader social relations of people in a community to the church, the marriage relationship, and the household, which includes children and slaves. In other words, all economic, legal, and public relations between people are to be subordinate to the core reality of love. In the same way, rules for the marriage and household, whether they are expressed in contemporary forms such as submission, obedience, and discipline, or in master/slave relations, are to participate in the formation of a social unity marked by love—that is, a family that is characterized by relations of love. Only such a quality of life begins to exemplify the quintessential aspect of all social relations, which is the very being of God as the true order of all created being.

It is difficult to understand why some are so reluctant to see the specific rules and regulations for family relationships as relative to the core structure of relationship itself. This is particularly so when it has been given such clarity in the person and work of Christ and reinforced with the command to be "imitators of God." The only reason can be that order is confused with regularity and rules, stability confused with rigidity, and the creative commandment of God confused with orders of natural creation. When this occurs, the freedom of God expressed through the contingent relation between created order and God's own absolute order of being will be misunderstood as "changing the rules." As a consequence, some will view the changing form of the family structure, including changing of role patterns, as disorder and disobedience. Careful reflection on Scripture should show the peril of this.

The conclusive evidence that the creative order is itself a formation of structure as a process is the eschatological orientation of the creative Word of God. Scripture always views the command of God as coming out of the future, so to speak. That is, it is the Word of God which is "coming" into being — not the past — that determines the present. The past is that which belongs to the present just to the extent that it too was called into being by the creative Word which is "coming." Thus, there is a continuity established between present forms and past forms through the stability and eternality of the creative Word. "Jesus Christ is the same yesterday and today and for ever" (Heb. 13:8); this is the testimony of faith, an echo of the name of God as the I AM, which is always to be understood as I WILL BE.

When the apostle Paul considers the significance of his own attempt to speak the commandment of God, he stops short of identifying his own teaching with God's command in a noncontingent way. Rather, he urges his hearers and readers to consider the eschatological orientation of both the teaching and the hearing of the Word of God. "Therefore do not pronounce judgment before the time," he writes, "before the Lord comes, who will bring to light the things now hidden in darkness and will disclose the purposes of the heart. Then every man will receive his commendation from God" (1 Cor. 4:5). But this has to do with authority, and we must now ask how we can understand the authority of the Word of God within this contingent and creative order.

CONVENTIONAL ORDER AND THE RENEWAL OF THE ROLE OF THE FAMILY

When modernity alters the traditional roles of society, particularly those of the family, it usually causes a reaction in the name of conservatism. Those who speak out against change in the role of the family, as well as against changing roles within the family structure, claim an authority based on the conventional order of tradition and time-tested values. These "values" are the abstract qualities of the good life, usually moral, which inhere in conventional life-styles. Thus, to alter the conventional roles is to challenge the intrinsic values of a society. In the final judgment, those who do so are considered to be immoral.

A moral authority then attaches itself to those who seek to uphold the conventional order of the family. It was, after all, the charge that his teaching corrupted the youth of Athens that brought Socrates to judgment by his peers, and led to his death. Because he questioned the traditional beliefs of his elders and encouraged young minds to question traditional authority as well, Socrates was charged with atheism and condemned to death.

It is but a short step from the charge that those who attempt to change the traditional, conventional order are violating a moral law to the charge that they are violating the law of God. Those who become the guardians of the moral order will also become the prophets of God. Thus, conservatism has always had a religious aspect to its passion.

When the family is held to be the cornerstone of a society, it becomes a quasi moral order of the society. That which is considered unconventional family life when measured by the traditional role of the family will then be subject to judgment. Traditionalists will attack the "new immorality" and issue a call for a return to the conventional to restore the "righteousness" of the nation. For example, the breakdown of moral authority in a society is often traced to a loss of parental authority in the home — specifically, the undermining of the male authority of the husband and father by the woman. Although she merely wishes to exercise her right to equality and full partnership in the marriage, she is seen as abandoning her "place" as wife and mother if she pursues activities and interests outside of the home. A woman who feels led to seek personal fulfillment beyond her role as wife and mother will find it difficult to account for the moral passion directed against her unless she understands the connection in the popular mind between conventional order and conventional morality.

All of this takes a more serious turn when Christians link conventional moral authority with scriptural authority. When the Bible itself is read as teaching an absolute order of role relationships within the family unit — "'Wives, be subject to your husbands" — failure to comply is tantamount to disobedience to God. For the evangelical Christian, who takes the Bible seriously as the inspired Word of God, the issue becomes critical. Biblical authority is, after all, a higher order of authority than conventional authority — we must obey God rather than men (Acts 5:29).

The issue of biblical authority narrows down to the issue of biblical interpretation. Given the assumption that the Bible speaks with the authority of God, an assumption shared by this writer, the question then becomes, What does the Bible teach concerning the family and roles within the family? Whatever assumptions one brings to the Bible will determine one's interpretations of the text. For example, one who holds that there is a fundamental natural order that is determinative of human existence in families will not permit the Bible to teach that which is contrary to the natural order. And when I say "not permit the Bible to teach," I mean only to suggest that we all read the Bible in an attempt to understand what it teaches, unless we adopt a sheer literalist approach to the language of Scripture, which is warned against within Scripture itself (see John 6:63). On the other hand, one who holds that order is indeterminate with regard to culture and nature will understand the teaching of the Bible to be relative and not absolute whenever it speaks in a cultural context. As a result, the interpreter is permitted to apply the teaching in a way that is consistent with the individual's own perceived good.

However, we have suggested that there is a third way of perceiving the structure of order when it comes to the family, and that is a created, contingent order. Here, we suggest, there are some positive implications for understanding how the authority of Scripture upholds the original and true order of the family while, at the same time, it does not fail to speak relevantly to each age. Just as the absolute, quintessential order is ascribed to God alone, even though it is embodied in a culturally relative social order, so the authority of God is embodied in Scripture, but not such that Scripture literally becomes God. That would be idolatry. Also, we saw that love is the material content of the inner structure of relations that constitute family. This is a love that first of all resides absolutely in God, and then, by his endowment, in humans who exist in his image and likeness. Relation, then, as we said, is the "logic of laws" that regulate family life and roles. The authority of the rules or laws that regulate life is a contingent authority. It is never found absolutely in the natural order, nor absolutely in the individual and personal order. It is a valid authority in its own right because it is divinely determined to uphold and support the true order of relation.

However, there is a hermeneutical principle, a principle of interpretation, that we must recognize at all times when we seek to understand the authority of natural order as contingent upon the divine order. We must always seek the "spirit within the words," to use the language of Jesus (John 6:63), or to seek the "logic within the rules," to use another metaphor. Significantly, in the same general context where Jesus earlier spoke of the distinction between spirit and word, he says, "Why do you not understand what I say [*lalia*]? It is because you cannot bear to hear my word [*logos*]" (John 8:43). The *logos* is the incarnate *Logos*, which is God and which has also become flesh (John

1:1, 14). Thus, the contingent and created order does have a point of interpretation common to both God as absolute and the created order as contingent upon the Creator. The authority of Scripture, therefore, is a contingent authority. Or rather, we should say, the authority of Scripture is based directly on the authority of God himself as he has given himself to be known and apprehended in the created order, which includes the language and written testimony of witnesses under the inspiration of the Holy Spirit.

In the context of the church, which is the community of Christian believers filled with the Spirit of Christ, the authority of Scripture anchors the life of the believer in the historical person and work of Jesus Christ. But because the church, as the new community of God and thus the new family of God, is formed through the presence and power of the resurrected Christ by his Spirit, the Scriptures are anchored in the contemporary presence and work of Christ through this community.

In this way we see that the original order of the family is grounded in the new family of God, and that the moral authority that upholds the order of the family as a social institution is grounded in the spiritual authority of love as expressed through Jesus Christ and as experienced in Christian community. The church, then, as the new family of God, demonstrates the authority of Scripture by renewing marriage and family where it has fallen into disorder, and by recreating marriage and family where it has been destroyed.

Here, then, is our agenda. We seek to set forth the basic structure of the quintessential order of the family as grounded in God's covenant love, experienced in good parenting, expressed through marriage, and culminating in spiritual maturity and the freedom of fellowship and participation in the church as the new family of God. And we do this with full confidence that the old commandment is also the new commandment.

PART TWO

COVENANT
AS A PARADIGM
OF THE FAMILY

CHAPTER THREE

BELONGING IS NOT A MATTER OF CHOICE

WHILE it is commonplace for social scientists to assert that human life is essentially social, they rarely agree on what constitutes the basis for this sociality. The philosopher John Macmurray attributes the origin of an explicit social theory to European intellectual history, in particular to that of the Greeks. Plato rejected the inherent dualism in the question posited by the Sophists, "Should men live by nature or by custom?" Instead, Plato responded, for men to live by nature is to live by custom, for human nature is social and custom is the bond of society.[1]

It was Aristotle who formulated the now classic saying "Man is a political [i.e., a social] animal." By this he meant that human beings exist in nature as members of a group, as do ants or bees. The unity that constitutes human community is the same, in principle, as that which constitutes the community of other creatures. The difference is one of complexity; and for Aristotle, this meant human rationality.

Macmurray traces two modern developments of this theory, the pragmatic and the idealistic, characterized by the thought of Hobbes and Rousseau, respectively. For Hobbes, persons who comprise society are by nature isolated units, afraid of one another and continuously on the defensive. However, since humans are rational, they recognize the universal and necessary means for realizing their own interests, for living a rational life. Thus an individual pragmatically forms unions with others that guarantee — in some measure, at least — the attainment of these long-term ends. Yet it is not a simple case of a person using all his powers to further his own interests; not only is he right in doing so, argues Hobbes, he is under obligation to a moral law to do so.[2] For the pragmatist, reason shows that it is to one's best interest to sacrifice momentary satisfaction and freedom for a greater long-term goal. The pragmatic mode of society is maintained by power, and it identifies society with the State, since

---

1. As noted by John Macmurray, *Persons in Relation* (London: Faber and Faber, 1961), p. 128.
2. Ibid., pp. 134-35.

the power of government is the necessary condition for the suppression of individual self-interest.

On the other hand, Macmurray states, the idealist concept of human society, as conceptualized and advocated by Rousseau, is based on the Romantic view that human nature is essentially positive and good. If the expressions of this nature are perverted it is because of the imposition of artificial social structures that prevent it from expressing itself freely. Consequently, Rousseau finds the bond of society in the human's "animal" nature, and the source of hostility and conflict he finds in reason. By unshackling human nature from these artificial devices and returning to the natural state of basically good human impulses, society will enter into its "golden age."[3]

We will not attempt to judge the validity of Macmurray's typology here but will point to his critique of both theories, which is helpful in our own search for a starting point. Both theories, argues Macmurray, are ambivalent expressions of the same negative motivation, which assumes that an impersonal connection, rather than a personal bond, lies between individuals. These social theories extrapolate from organic and impersonal views of human nature in an attempt to provide a basis for social relations. They fail precisely at this fundamental point, Macmurray charges, because the nature of persons is intrinsically communal, and not merely social.

Macmurray's view appears to agree with a biblical theology that locates the original form of the human in cohumanity. By cohumanity we mean a personal union in which differentiation into male and female becomes the expression of a life that is created after the divine image and likeness. This is most clear in Genesis 1 and 2, which sets forth the terms of human existence as both personal and communal in nature. It establishes the fact that solitary human existence is not good and therefore, it may be assumed, not actually attainable. Further, it shows the emergence of a social form of this cohumanity that involves an intentional movement from parenting to the creating of an entirely new and "supranatural" relation — marriage and family.

> Then the man said, "This at last is bone of my bones and flesh of my flesh; she shall be called Woman, because she was taken out of Man." Therefore a man leaves his father and his mother and cleaves to his wife, and they become one flesh. (Gen. 2:23-24)

Something is called "supranatural," of course, only if there is no natural law or principle that demands it or that accounts for it — it has no existence in nature as either principle or prototype. The prototype for this relationship between man and woman is the relation that God himself has with his people.

---

3. Ibid., pp. 140-41.

It is a covenant partnership that only subsequently is revealed to be a "sign" of the covenant relationship that Yahweh has with Israel, and that Christ has with the church. "The fact that man encounters woman — his wife — ," says Barth,

> means that he begins a new life with new ties instead of the old. He thus makes a break which is not self-evident. And in so doing he confirms everything which was said about the creation of woman and everything he had confessed in face of this finished divine work of creation. She is his "help-meet." Whatever his father and mother might be to him, they cannot be this. He remains their son, and must still honour them as his father and mother. But in the encounter and confrontation with his wife, he becomes a man.[4]

It is instructive, adds Barth, to note that Paul takes up this theme in Ephesians (5:29-30) in such a way that the "one flesh" created by this union is a sign of the relation of Christ to the members of the body, the church. Consequently, says Barth, "the basis of love and marriage is not, then, the creation of woman out of man, but behind and above creation the co-existence of Christ and his community. These are the 'great mystery' of Gen. 2."[5]

THE FAMILY AS PERSONAL, NOT MERELY SOCIAL

As we shall see, we cannot construe the formation of family as either a natural process that fulfills certain latent possibilities of creatureliness or a rational process by which that which is basically unnatural becomes humanized through socialization. In this sense we might say that the family, as God's command has determined it, is not intrinsically social but rather is essentially communal and, therefore, personal. The social structure of the family issues from its inherent communal and personal nature. But this is itself a result of a divine determination rather than of a creaturely orientation. The covenant partnership that God has established determines the existence of humanity in time and as a history. It is original, not consequential, to the existence of the human person as creature; that is, it presupposes creation and is present in the original form of creaturely humanity as the intrinsic structure of cohumanity as a social entity.

The term *family* originally denoted the retinue of servants who belonged to a master. Groups of fighters or actors are also called *familia*. In a broader sense, *family* became a comprehensive designation for a household, and only

---

4. Karl Barth, *Church Dogmatics*, ed. G. W. Bromiley and T. F. Torrance (Edinburgh: T. & T. Clark, 1936–1969), III/1, p. 328. Hereafter referred to as *CD*, with volume and part number.

5. Ibid.

subsequently — as is commonly understood today — did it come to mean clan, tribe, or, in a more restricted sense, a nuclear triad (mother, father, child[ren]). As Barth points out, "the ramifications of the family which are so important in the modern concept are not emphasised in the Old Testament, and even less so in the New."[6] The central focus of the Bible's view of the family is not on the family as a collective unit but on the relationship between parents and children. It is upon this relation that both the command and the promise rest. In other words, the parent/child relation is the core relation for the development of persons, not the concept of the family as a social construct. Developmentally, family can be viewed as a result and not a cause of personal life expressed as cohumanity. This, of course, is a somewhat artificial distinction, because parent/child and family coexist as social structures to some degree.

The point is that family as a social order cannot be posited as the original and creative course of the development of persons. To do so would be to revise Macmurray's typology, in which the personal is posited as a result of an impersonal order, either nature or reason. Rather, the development of persons begins with the affirmation and recognition of personal humanity. This is the function and responsibility of parents. Parenting cannot be accounted for by either nature or reason, but is accountable to the commandment of God by which human life is sustained and developed in its orientation toward fellowship with God himself.

Therefore, we must posit the development of persons as the original and creative source for the existence of family. Because parenting contextualizes and historicizes personal life, the family emerges developmentally as the result of parenting. While it is true that the relation of husband and wife ordinarily is established as a family unit prior to the role of parenting, this chronological order cannot be the basis for the actual order by which persons develop into family units. The reason for this is that before one can be an effective husband or wife one must have developed competence in covenant partnership through the experience of being parented. The legal marriage of a man and woman cannot create an "instant family." Rather, family is the result of an intentionality through which covenant partnership as a personal structure of being is now creatively exercised in such a way that a new unity of covenant partnership comes into being.

Where family is understood as the source of personal development, it is often viewed idealistically as a solution to a problem, or pragmatically as a means to an end. The enforced marriage of a pregnant teenager does not constitute a family, even though there will soon be both parents and a child. Recent studies have shown that within five years such marriages experience

---

6. *CD* III/4, p. 242.

an unusually high rate of separation and divorce. This is not to suggest that in many cases marriage is not desirable. The point, again, is that family is a result of a developmental process by which persons achieve competence in covenant-partnership relations; it is not the cause of such relations.

THE FAMILY AS COVENANT PARTNERSHIP

At this point we should clarify what we mean by *covenant*. In a technical sense, *covenant* in biblical theology means the unilateral relation established by God with his people Israel, through specific actions by which he summoned individuals and finally an entire nation into a history of response. Essential to this understanding of covenant is the concept of God's unilateral action by which the covenant comes into being and is sustained. The covenant, says Barth, "is the fellowship which originally existed between God and man, which was then disturbed and jeopardized, the purpose of which is now fulfilled in Jesus Christ and the work of reconciliation."[7]

While I do not intend to discuss the various theories on the concept of covenant in the Old Testament or to review the pertinent literature in biblical theology, a bit of background is helpful. Certainly, one cannot be as optimistic as were such earlier theologians as Eichrodt, who attempted to fit all of the Old Testament theologies into the single mold of covenant. It is now known that the earlier uses of the term in the Old Testament referred to the suzerainty relationships between a victorious nation and the conquered people. In this sense, a covenant was a treaty that was initiated unilaterally by the conquering leader to regulate the social and political life of the vassal. The terms of the treaty stipulated the responsibilities of the vassal, but also protected the rights of the people.

While there are several different types of covenants in the Old Testament, the foundational use of the concept is grounded in the Abrahamic covenant, by which God swore to make of Abraham a great nation. This covenant promise centered on the creation of a people of God through the generations of Abraham's descendants. Abraham's role was to believe in God's promise and to obey him through enacting the covenant sign of circumcision. The unconditional nature of the covenant as God established it entailed unconditional obedience, though the covenant itself was not conditional upon obedience. In other words, obedience to God cannot effect the covenant and disobedience cannot annul it. Israel's unfaithfulness to God's covenant love brought his judgment, but he did not annul the covenant.[8] According to T. F. Torrance,

---

7. *CD* IV/1, p. 22.
8. For an analysis of the biblical concept of covenant, see G. E. Mendenhall, "Covenant," in *The Interpreter's Dictionary of the Bible* (New York: Abingdon Press, 1962), 1:714-23.

In his covenant with Israel, God not only promised to be their God and required of them to walk before Him and be perfect, but gratuitously provided for Israel in the sacred cult the appointed way of response in fulfilment of His divine requirement. The prophets, some of whom came from the priesthood, insisted that this vicarious response had to be enacted by way of obedience into the life and existence of Israel in order to be efficacious reality, and pointed ahead to the Servant of the Lord as the chosen instrument for its actualization.[9]

Among the modern theologians, Karl Barth has done the most to promote the belief that the covenant is the fundamental order of God's relation to creation. According to Barth, we are not to view creation as having its own natural telos, with the covenant acting as a remedial institution because the creature has failed to live by this natural law. Rather, covenant itself is the inner and eternal presupposition of creation, while creation is the external and temporal manifestation of covenant.[10]

> God loves His own creature. This is the absolutely unique feature of the covenant in which His love is exercised and fulfilled. Its external basis, i.e., the existence and being of the creature with which He is covenanted, is the work of His own will and achievement. His creation is the external basis of this covenant. So firmly is this covenant established! So trustworthy is its presupposition not only on God's part but also on the part of the creature! So great is the faithfulness and constancy which it can as such expect from God in this covenant! And so transcendent is also the authority of the Founder of this covenant! . . . In this covenant God gives to it what He undertook to give to it when He first gave it its being and nature. And God wills from it as a partner in this covenant only that for which He prepared and bound and pledged it when He first gave it its being and nature.[11]

In this divine covenant, which is the presupposition of creaturely existence in human fellowship, God overcomes whatever negative or even indiscriminate tendencies there might be in creatureliness itself. Human existence is not a search for order and meaning amid confusion and chaos. Human relationships are not accidental or arbitrary. This is why the very first statement that places human existence within the creaturely realm involves intentionality and order. "Therefore a man leaves his father and his mother and cleaves to his wife, and they become one flesh" (Gen. 2:24). "Man's tearing himself away from his

---

9. T. F. Torrance, *God and Rationality* (London: Oxford University Press, 1971), p. 158.

10. *CD* III/1, p. 97. For an exposition of the theme of covenant in the theology of Karl Barth, see Stuart D. McLean, *Humanity in the Thought of Karl Barth* (Edinburgh: T. & T. Clark, 1981).

11. *CD* III/1, p. 96.

roots," says Barth, "must not be a rebellious self-emancipation, but the offering of the required sacrifice, the realisation of the autonomy attained and granted at this cost. He must not seek his I but his Thou—his 'help meet.' "[12]

The covenant partnership that will become visible in the relation between God and Israel is already the presupposition of the original union of man and woman. Barth adds,

> Love and marriage between man and woman become to them in some sense irresistibly a parable and sign of the link which Yahweh has established between Himself and His people, which in His eternal faithfulness He has determined to keep, and which He for His part has continually renewed. In this way they irresistibly see even this most dangerous sphere of human existence in its old and new glory.[13]

It is this fundamental relation between cohumanity as existence in marriage and the covenant between God and Israel that prompts us to see covenant as a paradigm of family. Thus, while the covenant partnership of the marriage and family relationship is but analogous to the covenant partnership between God and his people, it nonetheless is a fact of human nature. This correspondence between man's nature and God's nature, says Barth,

> does not give him any right or claim, any power to decide either to be or not to be the covenant-partner of God. It is no merit if he is ready to become this. He can only magnify the grace of God if he may do so. For it is only the grace of God if he is called and enabled to do so.[14]

Here we can readily see what a significant difference there is between contract and the biblical understanding of covenant. Contract, as James Torrance has helpfully pointed out, is based on mutual and bilateral terms. If one or the other defaults, the contract is broken and is no longer binding.[15] Covenant, on the other hand, is a unilateral relationship created and sustained by one party—God. Its source is in the unconditional election of God and it requires unconditional response. As the source of covenantal love and purpose, God remains faithful even where there is unfaithfulness in response. The covenant, therefore, has within itself the sources for its own renewal.

In a helpful discussion of the concept of covenant as a root metaphor, Stuart McLean suggests that we cannot reduce covenant to philosophical or social-theory options; rather, it contains within itself the components that are

---

12. Ibid., pp. 305-6.
13. Ibid., p. 315.
14. *CD* III/2, p. 321.
15. James B. Torrance, "Reformed Theology: A Critique of the Covenant Concept." Lecture at Fuller Theological Seminary, April 1975. Torrance is Professor of Systematic Theology, University of Aberdeen, Scotland.

often specified by such theories. According to McLean, covenant has seven discrete aspects: 1) its presupposition is community; 2) its basic unit is the dyad unit; 3) love is a struggle as well as harmony; 4) forgiveness; 5) bondedness is recovered; 6) law is essential, but relative; 7) the modes of time are juxtaposed.[16] Covenant partnership, therefore, best expresses this root metaphor in the structure of family, which is essentially social but, as we saw in Chapter One, finds its quintessential form in the particular quality of divine love that was expressed through redemptive history. God creates a partnership between Israel and himself. This partnership is unilateral in the sense that it is a gift from God, and yet it is a true partnership because it functions as a social dyad and enables bondedness to be experienced through struggle. Family members experience covenant partnership as a core experience, even though there are contractual relationships at varying levels.

It is with this perspective that we can finally say, with John Macmurray,

> The family is the original human community and the basis as well as the origin of all community.... The institutions by which society maintains itself are not natural; they are artifacts, and they are maintained by effort in order to sustain the personal life of men and women, and to prevent a relapse into the barbarism of a nearly organic life. Of these institutions, the family is the most primitive, the most persistent and the most fundamental.[17]

THE FAMILY AS
A PLACE OF BELONGING

To help us sharpen our focus on the concept of covenant as a theological paradigm of family, we will compare it with a more contemporary, ideological concept. Much of the modern literature concerning the family stresses its role as a quasi-democratic social institution. We are encouraged to think that a modification of the hierarchical, authoritarian structure of the family (represented by the dominance of parents over children) will result in a more egalitarian and democratic social unit. Further, we are told that freedom from authoritarian structures within the family will result in a sense of worth and importance on the part of each member. Ideologically, what is represented in this concept is the idea that the result of equality at the functional level of the social unit will be a feeling of personal value at the individual level.

Hence, parents are encouraged to include children in discussions involving

---

16. Stuart McLean, "A Functional-Relational Understanding of Covenant as a Distinctive Metaphor." Paper delivered at the Workshop on Covenant and Politics, Philadelphia, December 16, 1980. McLean is Associate Professor of Christian Education and Ethics, Graduate Seminary, Phillips University, Enid, Oklahoma.

17. Macmurray, *Persons in Relation*, pp. 155, 153.

the decisions that affect the welfare of the family unit. Consensus is sought through discussion, debate, and, finally, voting. Proponents of this form of "participatory democracy" suggest it as a way of equalizing the power base that naturally rests with those in the family unit who are older, stronger, and who control the resources by which the family lives. The "Father Knows Best" model gives way to "Eight is Enough"!

The basic assumption in this concept of social democracy is that equality is a fundamental right for human beings and that, consequently, equal participation in the outcome demands equal participation in the process. This means, however, that to deprive someone of participation is to cause the loss of that individual's personal value, no matter what the outcome of the process. In effect, this means that family life becomes highly politicized, with every aspect a negotiation for personal value in terms of participation in the process. And yet, it is argued, social existence is intrinsically a political existence, because every occasion of social interaction, even in family life, is a negotiation for the rights and values of one's own existence in community with, or at least in alliance with, other members of the social unit. Because the value of the person is what stands to be gained or lost in the negotiations, equality of personal position in the process becomes an absolute value. When parents surrender the decision-making power to the consensus of the family unit, children and young people in the family appear to be treated equally, and thus have full value as persons.

Certainly one would not want to argue that authoritarian parental dominance of children is better than the kind of participatory, consensus-seeking family life outlined above. There is much that is good in advocating greater sharing between all members of the family in the joys and sorrows, the difficulties and the rewards of family life. However, is equality in the sociopolitical process of family life the fundamental value of personhood? Or, to put the question another way, does one's value as a person depend more upon having the same share as everyone else or upon having a relationship in which one has an "only share"?

The point I am making here is that there is a distinction between the value that arises out of having a sense of uniqueness as a person and the value that emerges as a result of being treated equally as a person. Theologically, the premise of the concept of covenant is the exclusivity that the elected person (or people) has as a result of being "chosen." The ideological concept of equality is first of all an abstract value that begins with a certain indifference toward particularities that tend to exaggerate uniqueness. Only when each is treated the same, the argument goes, can one have full value. Those who have been excluded from equal treatment are denied their rights. Thus, while all are treated communally, all are in actuality denied any exclusive status. The covenant, on the other hand, begins with particularity and uniqueness as the source of personal value and practices indifference toward abstract and universal concepts of equality. This is a critical difference, and we need to explore it further in terms of the implications for our own approach to family life.

The basis of election and covenant in biblical theology is divine love. "The Lord your God has chosen you to be a people for his own possession, out of all the peoples that are on the face of the earth," wrote Moses. "It was not because you were more in number than any other people that the Lord set his love upon you and chose you ... but it is because the Lord loves you" (Deut. 7:6-8). This divine love is not subject to the judgment of abstract reason, which would demand "equal treatment" and all-inclusive participation. On the contrary, as Hans Urs von Balthasar argues,

> Only from the free uniqueness of God can an "exclusive" love between persons justify itself before the universal reason: ... if God is apparent as a free, personal being, then his appearance is in the manner of a free election, scandalous for all-leveling world-reason. In the center of the divine self revelation stands Yahweh's covenant with Israel: here abstracting man is trained in the fulfilling exclusivity of the relationship to God.[18]

One could paraphrase this to say that if God loved everyone equally, then he would love no one particularly. This is indeed scandalous! And it marks the sharp divergence of ideological value from a theological value. Theologically, love has its value in the uniqueness that results from "being chosen." Concern over what this means for others is irrelevant, as Peter discovered at the moment that he experienced the particular call, after the resurrection, to "follow me." Turning to his friend John, Peter asked the Lord, "What about this man?" And Jesus responded, "If it is my will that he remain until I come, what is that to you? Follow me!" (John 21:19-22). The basis for love, then, is not equality as an abstract and inclusive concept, but "being chosen" as a particular and unique relation to the one who loves. One could argue, then, that love as a concrete and specific experience of parenting results in persons who have a profound sense of their own value and thus are able to love others in the same sense. The principle of inclusion (and, subsequently, of equality) is subordinate to the reality of exclusivity in the form of electing love. Thus, covenant love aims at nurturing a sense of uniqueness rather than of equality or sameness.

The concept of uniqueness rather than equality is at the heart of the delightful story told by Antoine de Saint Exupery in his book *The Little*

---

18. Von Balthasar, *A Theological Anthropology* (New York: Sheed and Ward, 1967), pp. 187-88.

Prince.[19] The story is set in the Sahara Desert, where the narrator had landed his airplane when a mechanical problem forced an emergency landing. There he met an extraordinary little person who claimed to be from another planet scarcely larger than a house! The little prince, as the narrator called him, was extremely curious about the things on this planet earth.

One day, the little prince came upon a garden filled with roses in bloom. He was overcome with sadness, for on his little planet there was only a single rose, which had told him that she was the only one of her kind in all the universe. The little prince thought that he had been very rich, having a rose all of his own, which was unique in all the universe. Now he realized that he just had a common rose, similar to many others.

After this he met a fox, and asked the fox to play with him. "I cannot play with you," the fox said, "I am not tamed." The fox went on to explain:

> To me, you are still nothing more than a little boy who is just like a hundred thousand other little boys. And I have no need of you. . . . But if you tame me, then we shall need each other. To me, you will be unique in all the world. To you, I shall be unique in all the world.

"I am beginning to understand," said the little prince. "There is a flower . . . I think that she has tamed me." Going back to the rose garden, the little prince addressed them: "You are not at all like my rose," he said.

> As yet you are nothing. No one has tamed you, and you have tamed no one. You are like my fox when I first knew him. He was only a fox, like a hundred thousand other foxes. But I have made him my friend, and now he is unique in all the world.[20]

What the wise fox called being tamed, we understand as covenant love. This is not the indiscriminate love that first includes everything that is human in a social community, but the love that discriminates one from another as particular and unique. The argument that all must be treated equally in order that love be fair is ideological claptrap when judged by covenant love. The development of a strong sense of personal identity and value is a result of "being chosen" rather than of being considered equally with all others. It is the responsibility of parenting to love particularly, intentionally, and unconditionally. However, this does not mean that we must reject others so that this particular love of the one takes place — the doctrine of reprobation is not logically entailed in the doctrine of election. God does not need to create some for destruction in order to create others for salvation and life. Covenant love is discriminate and therefore unique precisely because it is intentional and

---

19. A. de Saint Exupery, *The Little Prince* (New York: Harcourt, Brace and World, Harbrace Paperbound Library, 1943).
20. Ibid., pp. 77, 80, 86.

unconditional. Abstract concepts of equality and fairness actually relativize the individual to the social group. Thus, the quality of divine love is not in its impartiality but in its partiality and its unconditional intentionality. "Men have forgotten this truth," said the fox. "But you must not forget it. You become responsible, forever, for what you have tamed."[21]

What covenant love teaches us is that we do not form our primary relationships through the mutuality of free will or choice, but our so-called choices are reinforced by our essential belonging. Michael Polanyi once put it this way: "Our believing is conditioned at its source by our belonging."[22] It is in "being responsible forever" that covenant love provides the basis for family. For this reason, family means much more than consanguinity, where blood ties provide the only basis for belonging. Family is where you are loved unconditionally, and where you can count on that love even when you least deserve it.

COVENANT AS
A PARADIGM FOR FAMILY

To this point we have only implied what it means to use covenant as a paradigm for family. As we work out a theology of the family, where theological insights are brought to bear on the nature and function of family, we need to draw out these implications, to give content to the form.

First, because covenant is the basis of family, *order precedes and overcomes disorder*. When viewed apart from covenant, creation appears as sheer randomness and capriciousness. Surely this is what caused Hobbes to postulate the pragmatic imposition of rational forms of power in order to preserve human existence from chaos. As we have seen, though, covenant is not a "rationalization" of disorder that God imposed as a consequence of sin and disorder. Rather, it is the original and divinely established intention by which creatureliness itself becomes an order of covenant partnership.

Covenant partnership, then, is a divinely determined order or existence for human beings. Genesis 2:24 places human existence within an order of cohumanity as the necessary and, therefore, logical result of the development of persons through the parent/child relation. The parenting relation is thus informed by the covenant/partnership relationship, from which it derives its goals and ends. Considered pragmatically, parenting may well be a desirable end. From the perspective of covenant, however, it is not a means to an end but the end itself.

---

21. Ibid., p. 88.
22. M. Polanyi, *Personal Knowledge* (London: Routledge and Kegan Paul, 1958), p. 322.

Practically speaking, we do not ordinarily enter into relationships that constitute family with a clear understanding of doing so because it is a "sign" of divine covenant. Our initial impulses are to some degree always either pragmatic or idealistic. Even our first parents were deceived by both idealism ("You shall be as God," said the serpent) and pragmatism ("it is desired to make one wise," thought the woman). In this regard, every act of human commitment carries an implicit inevitability of betrayal — not the betrayal of one person by the other, but the betrayal of our own intentions and commitments, the breaking of our vows when we meet frustration and failure. And so disorder enters where originally there was order. This is especially true if we view marriage and family as contractual and not covenantal, for then betrayal, or at least disillusionment, becomes factual and the union merely theoretical and finally unreal. Covenant partnership, however, is itself the basis for a true "disillusionment," where illusions have become the basis for motivations and actions. But the divine covenant-partner will permit no annulment of either his relation to them or their relation to one another. It is the reality of covenant that makes order the original reality and disorder only a deviation and distraction.

Yet covenant as the original order for marriage and family is not merely a fatalistic principle — "you made your bed, now lie in it" — but rather is itself a creative principle of renewal and recovery. For covenant is not that which assigns us to our past, but that which orients us to our future. To a certain extent, human covenant-partner relations are provisional as a social order. Even the customary words of the wedding vow echoes this fact — "till death do us part." Yet marriage and family are a "sign" of the covenant, and despite their provisional character as a social form, one cannot disregard this "order" without also contradicting the original and divine covenant-partner relation.

The second significance of covenant as a paradigm of family is that *selection is affirmed and sustained by election*. Because life appears to confront us with a random series of possible choices, any one of which can end up determining the course of our future, the possibilities can be quite paralyzing. Many of our selections, at the time just what we thought we wanted, have turned out to be disastrous. Our selections can also be quite demoralizing. As youngsters, most of us have had to suffer through the pain of being selected for something that did not interest us, whether it was as a dance partner or as a member of the "wrong" team in a pick-up game. One wonders how Eve felt on being presented to Adam as his "selection," when, as a matter of fact, there was no other alternative! In this case, certainly, selection *is* election — I choose you, and by my choice, you have no other choice!

Parenting is ordinarily nonselective. That is, we do not choose our parents, and if our parents choose to have a child, they are really electing to parent whatever child they receive through the apparently random process of genetic formation. In a sense, parenting is the affirming and sustaining of what appears to be the result of an indeterminate process. This is itself a "sign" of the covenant that is initiated by God's election of what, otherwise, would be an indiscriminate creature.

However, marriage and the creation of a family ordinarily do involve selection. Choices are made out of many possibilities for a mate. The temptation is great either to envision the ideal mate and project that ideal on a prospective partner, or to select a mate purely pragmatically (i.e., she has the values I want [or need] in a mate). Succumbing to either temptation, in my judgment, is the single greatest source of marital unhappiness.

It is helpful to remember that the basis for God's election of Israel was neither idealistic nor pragmatic. "It was not because you were more in number than any other people that the Lord set his love upon you and chose you, for you were the fewest of all peoples; but it is because the Lord loves you, and is keeping the oath which he swore to your fathers" (Deut. 7:8). God did not choose Abraham because he was the "right person," but once chosen, he became the "only person" through whom God would fulfill his covenant promise. For God, selection is invariable election. And the response then must either be to resist or to accept that election. That the elected may freely choose to resist is itself a mark of *God's* freedom and grace, not of one's natural rights or autonomy.

Our own creaturely humanity is more diffused than that. Covenant partnership is developmental in character. We discover our election in the process of our selections. Of course, there is more tolerance for error at some levels than at others; for example, to select some *thing* that appears beneficial to our life is less significant than to select some *person* for a lifelong mate. Good parenting is meant to assist us in accurately distinguishing between things and persons from the perspective of that which contributes essentially to the development of our own personal character as a covenant partner. Here, too, in the trial-and-error relationships involving companions and friends, there is a developmental process where, under proper guidance, we discern more accurately the different levels of relationship.

However, this experience not only gives us some skill in determining what is more appropriate and what contributes more genuinely to our own personal development but is also a process of discerning the reality of election as a confirmation and sustaining of our selecting and being selected. As we come to terms with the role of being parented, we are implicitly accepting election. One can oppose one's parents because of disagreements and even incompatibilities of style and temperament. However, within certain limits, one can develop into a mature covenant partner only by "honoring" one's parents as a sign of God's covenantal care and provision. The exceptions to this, of course, do not constitute an alternative model of parenting but rather testify to the distortions that are woven into the fabric of human existence. To become cynical and refuse to honor that which is not agreeable to one's own wants or needs is to distrust election itself. It is not difficult to see why children who grow up under such circumstances lack the competence to make good covenant partners in marriage and family relationships.

There is only a hint of the grateful recognition of election in the Genesis 2 account. When presented with the woman, the man responds, "This at last is bone of my bones and flesh of my flesh; she shall be called Woman" (Gen. 2:23). No other creature presented to Adam brought forth this response — each was only a possibility created to fill his need for companionship. God may have indeed summoned them forth out of the earth for Adam's consideration, but Adam demanded them and named them, exercising his own power of choice. But there is no such activity involved in the creation of the woman. The man is passive — rendered inactive by divine command. Upon awakening he recognizes the distinction between that which is for him because it is of him and that which can only serve him and can never be for him. Though clothed in mythical language, this story informs us of the original formation of humanity as covenant partnership. More than that, it expresses the joy at recognizing and accepting the election of God in that which is also selected.

Barth points out that the joy of fulfillment at the erotic level found in being a convenant partner is presented only twice in the Old Testament: Genesis 2 and the Song of Solomon. All other references to marriage and family, he says, are related to the problem and possibility of posterity, of human fatherhood, motherhood, the family, the child, and, above all, the son. In the Song of Solomon we see that the picture given in Genesis 2 is not just incidental or alien to the rest of the Old Testament. In this Song, says Barth, we see, from the standpoint of a woman, the completion of what the man utters in Genesis 2. Here we have the question of an incomparable covenant, of an irresistibly purposed and effected union. "I am my beloved's, and my beloved is mine" (Song of Sol. 6:3).[23]

What we discover — almost, as it were, by accident — in selecting a mate and in being selected is that God also participates in this selection by virtue of election. This is why the marriage vow is not itself capable of sustaining the relationship as the expression of human wisdom (in making the right choice) or of human endurance (I made the wrong choice, but I will see it through to the end). The marriage vow can be only a sign of the covenant, and those who make the vow can find lasting joy and love only in being covenant partners — receiving each other as God's elect.

---

23. *CD* III/1, pp. 312-15.

A third mark of the covenant upon the family is the fact that *faithfulness outlasts and overcomes faithlessness*. Throughout its description of Israel's tragic unfaithfulness and betrayal of covenant love, the Old Testament portrays God as a faithful spouse who will not abandon his beloved. In parable and in pronouncement the prophets summon Israel to consider the faithfulness of Yahweh who is espoused to Israel his bride. Unconditional love is the very core of the covenant relation between God and his people. Covenant partnership is God's determination that such unconditional love be experienced. As a sign of this covenant partnership, marriage and the family participate in the same unconditional character of love.

As part of this unconditional love one relinquishes the right to exist alone. Even as God relinquished this right in order to create and sustain a covenant partnership with his creature, so also must humans unconditionally relinquish this right in their original meeting and encounter.

Another aspect of this unconditional love is a commitment to the life of the other. Not only does one no longer have a right to exist alone, one now finds his or her own existence in the other. Moses was not averse to reminding even God of his unconditional commitment to share the life and destiny of his chosen people, those who bear his name (Exod. 32:11-14).

Also in this unconditional love is an acceptance of the gift of the other. All ethical obligation has its source in the love of neighbor (Rom. 13:10). This is an unconditional "debt" that we owe one another. It is this debt that God assumes in entering into covenant partnership with his own creatures.

The covenant is exclusive as well as inclusive. It excludes all that stands against the determination of covenant love itself. But it also includes, unconditionally, all that belongs to covenant love. Undoubtedly a shadow always lies over the human dimension of covenant partnership. Inconstancy and unfaithfulness shadow every human relationship. We cannot purge this alien possibility by either religious or humanistic idealism. But all this, says Barth,

> far from altering, proves finally even in its negativity that the covenant, as God willed, concluded and now maintains it, is a covenant of love and marriage. Love is always love even if it is not deserved or reciprocated by the beloved, even if she rejects and disgraces it by unfaithfulness. Similarly, marriage is always marriage even though broken by Yahweh's partner. Yahweh is always the Lover, Bridegroom and Husband. And His lost people is always His beloved, His bride and His wife.[24]

---

24. Ibid., p. 316. Cf. Jeremiah 3:12; 4:1; Ezekiel 16:59-60; Hosea 2:16-17; 2:19-20; Isaiah 54:5-8.

As the fundamental basis for marriage and family, covenant partnership is tough and unrelenting when confronted with disappointments and even unfaithfulness. The first sign of a contradiction in committed relationships is not the end but the beginning of covenant love. Covenant partnership is also resourceful and hopeful. Where dead ends and repeated failures occur, a new pilgrimage can take place. Because the covenant exists only provisionally in terms of social and temporal institutions and traditions, it can leave its own ruins without leaving anything of significance behind. Many a marriage has experienced the demolition of its walls, which were carefully built both idealistically and pragmatically. Those who are prepared to be covenant partners and have indeed entered into the creation of marriage and family will not long be detained by such ruins, but will continue to build a new style and a new place.

No social institution has the resources for such endurance and renewal. For this reason the family as constituted by the covenant love of God is the source of renewal and stability for society. Yet the family must "grow its own" members through the development of persons capable of covenant partnership. Thus it turns out that the parenting process is original to the building of strong families. God is the parent who loves before he is the covenant partner, and so it is with parenting that the paradigm continues to unfold.

CHAPTER FOUR

TOGETHER IN COVENANT

C ARL Whitaker, the eminent psychiatrist from the University of Wisconsin Medical School, is one of those rare mental-health professionals who has traveled the intellectual road leading from an emphasis upon linear and individual explanations of human behavior to a more systemic approach.[1] One of his views can be summed up by his statement, "I don't believe in divorce. Not on religious grounds, but on the grounds that divorce just doesn't exist. You can fall into love but you can't fall out. Once you have made a commitment to another, that commitment is irrevocable. You can't undo what you've done."[2]

In other words, says Whitaker, relationships within the family involve an irrevocable investment of affect — one's conscious, subjective emotions. Just as in legal usage an irrevocable trust is one in which property can be given to heirs for their use but the heirs cannot divest themselves of the property lest it revert to another, so it is within the family. The peculiar nature of affect within family relationships is such that the trust associated with its deposit in the life and experience of those involved cannot be broken. That is, it cannot be made void or canceled. The trust can be disrupted; it can become dysfunctional and destructive. But, according to Whitaker, it can never cease to exist. The affect will always persist. In this sense a husband will always be a husband and a wife will always be a wife even if there has been a divorce. Whitaker, it should be noted, is not against the practice of divorce. What is important, however, is that a person cannot pretend that the first relationship ever stops existing. When there has been a death or a divorce one must make a new life based upon the realities of the past, with all of the attending and residual "investments."

Whitaker illustrated his position with a reference to adoption. As he pointed out, adoption can be particularly difficult if the reality of this irrevocable deposit of affect between the child and the natural mother is not fully taken into account. The fact is that a child forever carries within himself or herself the affective deposits of his or her relationship with the natural mother.

---

1. See *From Psyche to System: The Evolving Therapy of Carl Whitaker*, ed. John R. Neill and David P. Kniskern (New York: The Guilford Press, 1982).
2. Carl Whitaker, Seminar on Family Therapy, presented at Los Angeles, December 1-2, 1979.

However soon after birth the child may have been adopted, the fact of the relationship between the child and the mother *in utero* cannot be denied.

As the executive director of an adoption agency for nine years, I have also observed what Whitaker is talking about. In particular, I have noted a significant difference between those families whose adopted children grew up with little or no trauma associated with the issue of adoption and those families which struggled with the constant fear or rejection of the child's relationship with its birth-parent. When it came time to tell the child that he or she was adopted, those families which accepted the fact of the adoption and the reality of the child's relationship with the birth-mother evidenced the least trauma and anxiety over the disclosure. On the other hand, those families which tried to deny or disparage the child's birth relationship struggled most with the issue.

In other words, when bonding occurs between human persons, even at the earliest and most primitive levels, an irrevocable deposit of affect occurs. It cannot be denied.

The same can be said for the children of divorce. A stepmother or stepfather can never replace the natural parent. He or she can be a substitute — often providing an even healthier and more stable atmosphere — but never a replacement. Even though some natural relationships are destructive, the bonding has taken place. The relationship between the child and the stepparent, however, must develop its own deposit of affect. And when that relationship embraces the dimension of commitment another "covenant" is born.

What is of special importance in the development of a theology of the family is the nature of this relationship between bonding and affect. I would suggest that the essence of this relationship constitutes the essence of the nature of covenant — or commitment, as it is known in the literature of the social sciences. Covenant or commitment is something you give to another that cannot be taken away once it is given. In fact, I believe that this irrevocable deposit of affect we theologically call covenant and sociologically call commitment is the linchpin for a theology of the family. It is the overarching theme that binds a theology of the family together.

Family relationships, whether parent/child, husband/wife, brother/sister, or any other special bonding relationship, are reflections of the covenant relationships that exist within the Godhead and are reflected in the relationship between God and humankind and between human persons as they are created "in the image of God." This "image" reflects the nature of the persons as well as their relationship. Covenant is represented by the "and" in the equations "God and man," "man and woman," and "parent and child."[3] The dynamics of

---

3. For further discussion see Dennis B. Guernsey, *A New Design for Family Ministry* (Elgin, IL: David C. Cook, 1983).

covenant are, in fact, the system dynamics of the relationships called family, whether we are talking about the family of God or the families of human persons.

I have suggested that the sociological equivalent to the theological concept of covenant is the concept of commitment. Sociologists have long viewed this concept as central to the understanding of courtship and marriage. The problem is that as a concept it has most often been vaguely defined and thus has been inadequately researched. For example, the Theodorsons, in their dictionary of sociological terms, used the term to mean "a feeling of obligation to follow a particular course of action."[4] Others, struggling with a definition of the term, have extended the concept to the point that they have generated a whole literature on commitment.[5]

DIMENSIONS
OF COMMITMENT

Part of the problem with understanding commitment is the commonsense meaning of the term. M. P. Johnson posits that *commitment* most often conjures up "images of dedication and personal determination, to the neglect of nonpersonal factors which might commit one to a line of action."[6] Thus, *commitment* becomes a personal term rather than a social or structural one. This focus on the personal has resulted in the joining of the term in courtship and marriage research with the terms *attraction* and *satisfaction*. The subtleties attached to defining the term personally rather than socially or structurally result in equating a loss of attraction or satisfaction with a loss of commitment. Defining the concepts in terms of one another soon leads to the belief that to diminish the importance of one is automatically to diminish the other. That is, if we define *commitment* personally and take it to be just another way of

4. G. A. and A. G. Theodorson, *A Modern Dictionary of Sociology* (New York: Thomas Y. Crowell, 1969), p. 56.

5. Cf. P. Abramson, H. R. Cutler, and R. W. Kantz, "Social Power and Commitment," *American Sociological Review* 23 (Feb. 1958): 15-22; H. S. Becker, "Notes on the Concept of Commitment," *American Journal of Sociology* 66 (July 1960): 32-40; D. G. Dean and C. P. Spanier, "Commitment: An Overlooked Variable in Marital Adjustment," *Sociological Focus* 7 (1974): 113-18; J. DeLamater, *The Study of Political Commitment* (Washington, D.C.: American Sociological Association, 1973); J. R. Eshleman and J. N. Clarke, *Intimacy, Commitments, and Marriage: Development of Relationships* (Boston: Allyn and Bacon, 1978); C. W. Hobart, "Commitment, Value Conflict, and the Future of the American Family," *Journal of Marriage and Family* (Nov. 1960): 405-12; M. P. Johnson, "Commitment: A Conceptual Structure and Empirical Application," *Sociological Quarterly* 14 (1973): 395-406; and C. A. Kiesler, *The Psychology of Commitment* (New York: Academic Press, 1971).

6. M. P. Johnson, "Personal and Structural Commitment: Sources of Consistency in the Development of Relationships," Department of Sociology, The Pennsylvania State University, 1978.

saying *attraction* or *satisfaction*, then if there is a loss of attraction or satisfaction in a marriage there must of necessity be a loss of commitment. Given the first, the second must follow. What began as a definition for use in the literature soon changes the meaning of the term itself. The definition becomes the justification for assuming an issue — such as divorce — to be a given.

However, it is not necessary to make commitment only personal or to equate it with attraction or satisfaction. According to H. S. Becker, it is possible for a person to initiate or sustain a line of action regardless of his or her personal feelings about it.[7] Johnson further develops Becker's position.[8] He says that strong attachment to a person or an object can lead to a particular line of action. We can refer to this attachment as "personal commitment." Examples of this are such statements as "She's committed to him" or "He's committed to preaching the gospel." In this sense *commitment* is taken to mean the internal cognitive and affective energy needed to initiate or sustain a course of action. It is dependent upon the values and beliefs of the individual. It is a reflection of his or her attachment to a person or to an object.

There is, however, another dimension to the concept of commitment, which can be illustrated by the phrase, "He can't back out now. He's committed himself." According to Johnson, "the connotation here is one of external constraints which arise as a direct consequence of the initiation of a line of action and which make it difficult to discontinue it should one's sense of personal commitment decline." He calls these constraints "structural commitments." Stated succinctly, structural commitments are "events or conditions which constrain the individual to continue a line of action once he or she has initiated it, regardless of his or her personal commitment to it."[9]

Johnson outlines four kinds of structural commitments that one may engage in once one initiates a line of action. (Note the similiarity to Whitaker's position.) They are:

1. Termination procedures. Such procedures would involve a disproportionate cost as compared with what is gained. If the costs of termination outweigh the gains then the relationship is not terminated irrespective of the loss of personal attraction or satisfaction.

2. Irretrievable investments. Once something is invested, such as affect, time, or money, it cannot be retrieved. The thought of losing the investment outweighs the loss of attraction or satisfaction.

3. Social pressures. Others build patterns of behavior around our lines of actions. They take us into account when they make their plans and they expect us to take them into account when we make ours. Social pressure in marriage

---

7. Becker, "Notes on the Concept of Commitment," pp. 32-40.
8. Johnson, "Personal and Structural Commitment."
9. Ibid.

relationships results when the norms regarding permanence are extended to the various commitments that surround the relationship. When that happens social pressure becomes a dimension of structural commitment. This reality prompted Margaret Mead to argue for "marriage in two steps." That is, to diminish the social pressures upon the young, inexperienced newlyweds faced with the "forever" of commitment, Mead proposed a trial period before the second, permanent step. Reducing the social pressure on the couple during the first period would, according to Mead, increase the likelihood that the second would be more permanent.[10]

4. Available alternatives. This function of structure is explained in terms of the perceived available alternatives.[11] What is "out there" may not be as attractive as what is "in here," even if what is "in here" has lost its attractiveness.

In summary, Johnson suggests the following:

> A full account of commitment processes must attend to the social processes which produce events which make it difficult for individuals to change their behavior, and to the manner in which such commitments affect the cognitive processes of the individuals involved.[12]

What are those "commitment processes" that bring about both personal and structural commitment when applied to the creation of a theology of the family? I suggest that for the Christian, being "together in covenant" constitutes the biblical structural commitment that persists during those times in a marriage and family when the dimensions of personal attraction and satisfaction wane. To have lost the meaning of covenant is to have lost the meaning of commitment. Likewise, to have lost the structure of covenant is to have abandoned family relationships to the capriciousness of the personal, to the ebb and flow of hair lines, waist lines, bust lines, and so forth. Our society becomes one of serial nonbinding personal commitments based upon the time of the month or the time of life. There must be something more. And there is: it is to recapture for ourselves and for one another the fullness of the doctrine of covenant.

THE MEANING OF COVENANT

According to James Torrance, a covenant is "a promise binding two people or two parties, to love one another unconditionally."[13] It is the most fundamental

---

10. Margaret Mead, "Marriage in Two Steps," *Redbook*, July 1966, 48ff.
11. J. Thibault and H. H. Kelley, *The Social Psychology of Groups* (New York: John Wiley and Sons, 1959).
12. Johnson, "Personal and Structural Commitment."
13. James Torrance, "Reformed Theology: A Critique of the Covenant Concept." Lecture presented at Fuller Theological Seminary, April 11, 1975.

statement of relationship that exists. It is the nature of the relationship between God and man, between husband and wife, between parent and child.

As mentioned in the previous chapter, the concept of covenant is in contrast to the concept of contract, which is "a legal relationship in which two people or two parties bind themselves together on mutual conditions to effect some future result."[14] The significant difference between the two is that the relationship between God and his people is always covenantal and never contractual. The covenant or agreement of relationship is unilateral. God, and God alone, passed through the middle of the sacrifice as he committed himself to Abraham (Gen. 15). God and God alone sacrificed his Son on the cross for the sins of humankind. The mentality of covenant is that "I commit myself to do or to be for you whatever I have agreed to do or to be because of my commitment." The commitment becomes a structure in and of itself.

What is of interest to our discussion is the parallel between Johnson's concept of personal commitment and Torrance's concept of contract. Personal commitments can ebb and flow according to the personal attractiveness of or the satisfaction with a particular relationship. The personal involves "mutual conditions." If either you or I cease or fail to meet the conditions of the relationship as it was previously agreed to, then my commitment is likely to diminish. In contrast, a structural commitment maintains a line of action that makes it difficult to discontinue the commitment even if the personal commitment declines. Such is the stuff of covenant, or, rather, the opposite: covenant is the stuff of structural commitment.

CONCLUSION

The purpose of the two chapters in this section has been to establish the importance of covenant as a unifying theme for a theology of the family. Such a theme has a rich tradition in the literature of both theology and the social sciences. What is of equal importance, however, are the pragmatics of the issues. We live in a time of personal drift marked by throw-away relationships, by transience, and by terrible impermanence. Nothing lasts. We seem to have accepted "planned obsolescence" as the norm. It has become "right" that all things destruct after 50,000 miles. The zeitgeist has become the mentality of the contract, and our contracts are written on the backs of paper napkins from fast-food chains. We enter into and exit from relationships as if they were McDonald's restaurants. We have come to relate to each other so casually that being in family with one another has about the same relationship as a Big Mac has to french fries and a medium Coke.

---

14. Ibid.

The greater tragedy is that we as Christians seem to have capitulated to such a mentality almost as if it were a given. The alternative to the unfettered freedom of the individual to do his or her own thing is held out to be a terrible binding legalism. While it is true that we are not justified by works, it is also true that grace has its obligations, which of necessity are a limitation to freedom. But as it is with us and God when we accept the unconditional gift of his Son, grace has its costs. So it is with human relationships patterned after grace. They are intended to be unconditional. They are meant to be forever. But they have their obligations, which persist even when the attraction and the satisfaction have ebbed. "Hang in there, baby" is more than pop psychology on a poster.

PART THREE

PARENTING
AND THE DEVELOPMENT
OF PERSONS

CHAPTER FIVE

GROWING UP IS CHILD'S PLAY

I N every hour the human race begins."[1] This is all too easy to forget in the midst of a world history that appears to stretch back into the primitive, and yet recognizably human, world of antiquity. Nor is it any easier to remember in the ongoing and seemingly inevitable rush of humanity out of the present and into the future. We do not really believe that the human race begins with our birth. But the fact that it begins with a birth is undeniable. And in a certain sense it is also true of us—our birth was the birth of the human race. In each of us it begins anew. That which has never been now comes into existence in the myriad of human faces that emerge breathlessly out of darkness into light. With its very first breath, a human life begins the adventure of becoming human. And despite the perils of this adventure, with its many tears and trials, it is, for the most part, considered to be preferable to its only alternative.

It is not the purpose of this chapter to establish what is meant by that which is human as contrasted to the nonhuman. Our concern is more with the process by which that which is human *becomes* human. What we propose is more developmental than foundational. Theological anthropology's task is to set forth the form of the human;[2] our task is to trace out, in at least a tentative manner, the formation of the human, given certain theological assumptions.

THE FORMATION OF HUMAN PERSONS

Human personhood certainly is a mystery—not only a question of why there should be persons at all, but a fundamental mystery in the experience of one's

---

1. Martin Buber, *Between Man and Man* (London: Collins, Fontana, 1961), p. 109.
2. For an extended discussion of theological anthropology, in which the form of the human is developed, see Ray S. Anderson, *On Being Human* (Grand Rapids: Eerdmans, 1982), chaps. 1-5. See also the recent work by Wolfhart Pannenberg on the nature of persons as social beings, *Anthropology in Theological Perspective*, trans. Matthew J. O'Connell (Philadelphia: Westminster Press, 1985). Particularly helpful is the section entitled "The Human Person as Social Being," pp. 157ff., and his discussion of the "we preceding the I" in the development of personhood, pp. 408ff.

own personhood as well as in experiencing the other as person. True, there is less naivete today concerning the multifaceted phenomenon of human personhood; our scientific prowess has probed into the deepest recesses of the human experience and offered explanations for what used to be considered the influence of either angels or demons upon human personalities. But with less naivete there is no reason why there should be less mystery, for mystery is the threshold of the personal set within the concrete structures of physical existence. Without the mystery of human personhood, love and relationship would be little more than an organic "chip" on which all the microscopic connections are "wired" in such a way that predictability insures increasing efficiency in mating as well as meeting. Martin Dysart, the psychiatrist in Peter Shaffer's powerful play, *Equus*, says,

> A Child is born into a world of phenomena all equal in their power to enslave. It sniffs — it sucks — it strokes its eyes over the whole uncomfortable range. Suddenly one strikes. Why? Moments snap together like magnets, forging a chain of shackles. Why? I can trace them. I can even, with time, pull them apart again. But why at the start they were ever magnetized at all — just those particular moments of experience and no others — I don't know. And nor does any one else. Yet, if I don't know — if I can never know that — then what am I doing here? And I don't mean clinically doing or socially doing — I mean fundamentally! These questions, these Whys, are fundamental — yet they have no place in a consulting room.[3]

In asking such questions one has passed over the threshold of the impersonal to the personal, from the nonhuman to the human, and from that which is merely creaturely to a human form of creatureliness. There are certain assumptions that we must now make clear as we proceed to develop a model of parenting that assists in the formation of human persons.

The first assumption is that *creatureliness is a necessary but insufficient condition for human existence.* One cannot be human without also necessarily being a flesh-and-blood creature placed somewhere on the continuum that makes up the life of all creatures. Human persons may not develop out of sheer creatureliness, but they do develop as creatures as well as persons. Therefore, those creaturely aspects of existence that humans share with nonhuman creatures are essential to the development of the person. This assumption entails the fact that the uniqueness of the human creature results from a determination that has its source outside of the creaturely realm. That is, the form of the human is determined by that which is transcendent to creatureliness — there is no telos hidden within sheer creatureliness that can reach beyond the limits of creatureliness itself to give form to the human. The

---

3. Peter Shaffer, *Equus* (New York: Avon Books, 1974).

impersonal does not contain within itself the source of the personal—though the reverse may well be true. Theologically, this transcendent source is understood to be the creative power of the Word and Spirit of God. There is, then, a contingent relation between creatureliness and humanity. The human creature, in its personal existence, must be sustained by something—some personal reality—beyond its own creaturely existence.

Second, we should note that *human existence is originally social and only consequentially psychological*. This assumption entails the conclusion that individuality as a particular experience of self-awareness, with its attendant psychological manifestations, derives from an experience of unity and relation with others. In the creation account in Genesis 2, the solitary human is under the divine judgment—it is not good to be alone. Only when there is a complementary experience of humanity in terms of what we might call cohumanity does the form of the human appear actually—not merely potentially—complete. The "we" exists before the "I," or, one could say, the "I" does not exist except as it is contained in the "thou." The implications of this assumption will become quite striking when we turn later to consider the development of personhood through the social structure of the family.

The third assumption we need to consider is that *existence as person derives from existence in relation*. This, of course, logically follows the previous assumption. To attribute the quality of "personal" to creaturely being is to denote being that is differentiated in its unity in such a way that "relationship" takes place as a manifestation of being. Theologically, this is what is meant by asserting that human persons are created in the "image and likeness of God" (Gen. 1:26-27). It is this aspect of being the image and likeness of God that differentiates between human and nonhuman creatures, by determining their relation to God as Creator and Lord. That is, one can make the formal distinction between human and nonhuman creatures only by recognizing the distinction between created human persons and God the Creator. Without this formal distinction as a theological assertion, distinctions between human and nonhuman creatures would be relativized to the variations that occur on the continuum of creatureliness itself.

The material aspect of that image and likeness is the differentiation within the human, or between human persons, manifested concretely as male or female. Here we see why the differentiation between God and the solitary human, as well as the differentiation between the solitary human and other creatures, though formally made in Genesis 2, had no material actuality in terms of the differentiation within the human experience itself. Only when this material differentiation became an actuality for the man and the woman did the formal differentiation have any meaning. Personal being, at the human level, is necessarily constituted to be male or female being, not because the physical or creaturely aspect of sexual differentiation has the power to create personal being, but because the material content of personal being first of all takes place as creaturely being before it can be considered as an abstract or formal possibility. In this case, the sexual differentiation, which humans share with other nonhuman creatures, becomes the sign of the personal differentiation that constitutes human being.

The final assumption is that *human being, as differentiated from non-human creatureliness, is being that is characterized by openness toward the power that constitutes it.* That is, the openness of being that is characteristic of the human is what constitutes the freedom of being that is unique to humans. Theologically, we understand this as the spiritual dimension of human existence. The basic unity of the body/soul duality is endowed with spirit in such a way that there is a spiritual openness toward other beings. This is the quintessence of personal being, which locates the spiritual dimension of human life directly at the core of personal existence. This assumption will have telling significance when we discuss the matter of spiritual formation and the family.

Because God the Creator, who endows human existence with spiritual life, not only accompanies the human person in the process of becoming a person but stands ultimately as the source of that becoming, there is an eschatological orientation to human existence. The Greek word *eschatos* denoted that which is last, or at the end of the process. In this sense, personhood moves toward a goal that at the same time is the source of that movement. This is the sense in which one can say that in becoming a person, one becomes what one already is, by virtue of the original divine determination. Yet this does not result in a biological or natural determination that would eliminate the freedom of the person to become through an experience of the self to others. Rather, this process of becoming what one actually is — a complete human person — is also a real process with real possibilities of success and failure. This is due to the freedom of God, not to the autonomy of the human self. God's freedom means God's participation in life and in the structures that bring about and assist human life in its becoming.

In summary, we may say that the form of the human is social, personal, sexual, and spiritual. It is not clear that there is an order arising from the sequence in which they are listed, although it would not be surprising to find that there is. Developmentally, it may be that experiences that produce authentic sociality lead to clarification of one's identity at the personal and sexual levels, with spirituality the concluding and integrating factor in achieving mature personhood. But this is an inconclusive — although interesting — hypothesis at this point.

DEVELOPMENTAL ASPECTS
OF PARENTING

Our discussion so far has been at the purely theoretical level. At the practical level, becoming human is a process that begins at birth and continues, more or less, until one's creaturely life is ended. It is to this process that we now turn our attention. While our perspective continues to be theological, we can look at the process itself quite straightforwardly as a process in which the social and behavioral sciences have an equally vested interest, as does theological science. It is my hope that this discussion of parenting will help us to form a developmental model for becoming mature human persons that integrates a theological perspective with the other behavioral disciplines.

"The mother-child relation," says John Macmurray, "is the original unit of human existence."[4] I would prefer to substitute "parent" for "mother." This is not to suggest that mothers can or ought to be replaced, but that parenting — not mothering — represents more precisely the basic social structure in which human existence originates.

The physical or biological process through which children are brought into the world cannot alone account for the oversight and responsibility for parenting children. At present (although one cannot say how much longer), children come into the world through the biological process of conception and birth, involving both a mother and a father. Should it come to pass that the father is thought of more as the "donor" and the mother the "carrier," it nonetheless remains a creaturely function. Physical paternity surely entails what parenting means by way of accountability for the development of human life, but it cannot of itself, as a creaturely act, totally account for the responsibility of parenting.

According to Karl Barth, it is the historical order, not the physical, that constitutes the demand of parenthood.[5] By history, of course, Barth means that which takes place under the determination of the Word of God in its particularity and uniqueness. Thus, parenthood is accountability to the command of God, not merely to the necessity of physical and creaturely existence. The commandment to honor one's parents does not mean the submission of one who is weak and helpless to one who is stronger and older. Rather, it is the recognition that these particular "elders," who brought us into physical existence, bear on our behalf the commandment of life, which is also the promise of life, as determined by relation to the Word of God. This responsibility, of course, can be borne by other than biological parents in exceptional

---

4. John Macmurray, *Persons in Relation* (London: Faber and Faber, 1961), p. 62.
5. *CD* III/4, p. 243.

cases. And, as we shall see, it can be borne by one of the biological parents in cases where it is impossible for both to do so.

In further qualifying what is meant by the concept of parenting, we must add that, although the parent may fulfill the role of educator, parenting is more than educating. If educating presupposes an originative or creative instinct in the child that can be developed and trained, parenting assumes an instinct for communion that can be called forth and affirmed. "What teaches us the saying of Thou," says Martin Buber, "is not the originative instinct but the instinct for communion."[6] This instinct for communion is stronger than "libido"; it is the longing for the world to become present to us as a person. The educator summons into existence latent creative powers, which may or may not result in the development of persons into mature humanity. The parent, however, summons the latent mystery of the "I" into relation, which is a summons into responsibility, into communion. Thus, parenting is necessarily humanizing when it takes place under the divine commandment, while educating may or may not be.

For example, a physical therapist can "educate" the muscles and nervous system in such a way that coordination and movement is possible. This type of education also takes place with nonhuman creatures. In the same way, one might suggest that a psychotherapist can "educate" through a stimulus-response mechanism in such a way that desired behavioral change is effected. But is this, too, not basically a creaturely and prehuman process? In this sense, education may fulfill certain limited goals without yet fulfilling the role of parenting.

It is for this reason that we have resisted the temptation to speak of family as the original structure that determines human existence. The concept of family derives from the concept of parenting and is dependent upon it for its significance in regard to the development of persons. "The ramifications of the family which are so important in the modern concept," says Karl Barth, "are not emphasised in the Old Testament, and even less so in the New."[7] The family as a collective unit is not the center of focus in the Bible. Rather, the relation of parents and children is central, and it is upon this relation that both the command and the promise rest.

In focusing upon the parent/child relation, we are not disregarding the other significant relations that a child experiences; namely, sibling relationships and relationships with other members of the extended family, such as grandparents, aunts and uncles. These other relationships are subsumed under

---

6. Buber, *Between Man and Man*, p. 114.
7. *CD* III/4, p. 242.

the category of parent/child and are basically ancillary, although by necessity they also may become surrogate.

Theologically, parenting has its antecedent in the Old Testament concept of the Fatherhood of God. According to Ephesians 3:15, God is the Father of whom the whole family in heaven and on earth is named. In Isaiah 63:16, appeal is made to God as Father beyond all human fathers: "For thou art our Father, our Redeemer from of old is thy name." Jesus accentuates this when he warns, "And call no man your father on earth, for you have one Father, who is in heaven" (Matt. 23:9). And Israel is continually reminded that she exists solely by a fatherly action of God: "Do you thus require the Lord, you foolish and senseless people? Is not he your father, who created you, who made you and established you?" (Deut. 32:6). "Know then in your heart that, as a man disciplines his son, the Lord your God disciplines you" (Deut. 8:5; cf. Deut. 1:29-30; Hosea 11:1; Jer. 3:19-20).

Human parents stand in a relation to their children in a way analogous to the way in which God is related to his people, as Father.[8] The seniority of parents over their children is relative, not absolute. Also, both parents, the mother and father, equally bear the responsibility of fulfilling, by analogy, that which is represented by the Fatherhood of God. That is, it is impossible, from a theological perspective, to equate the male role in parenting with the concept of God as Father. Whatever distinctive aspects belong to the male role of parenting, they must be established on other grounds. God's Fatherhood includes all of the nuances of parenting represented by analogy in human parents. For example, both nurture and discipline, both compassion and chastisement are exemplified by the Fatherhood of God, as generally portrayed in the Old Testament.

Everything said thus far implicitly assumes that personhood, or selfhood, is as much a result of as it is an originally given determinant of human existence. The formal truth that supports this assumption is contained in the assertion that humanity as personal selfhood is experienced as cohumanity. In naming the animals, Adam could not "parent" the beasts of the field in such a way that they became more and more human. There was apparently no "givenness" with regard to human selfhood in their nature. Yet in "naming" the woman as his copartner, the man discovered and experienced the openness of his own being to another. It is in this structure of cohumanity and as a consequence of this experience that he "became a person." In this developmental concept of personal human existence, the role of the significant other is much more than pedagogical, it is ontological. That is, the being of one is opened up and affirmed by the being of the other. For this reason we can state

---

8. Cf. ibid., pp. 246-47.

as a formal truth that the ontological determination of human selfhood in one person lies with the openness of being on the part of another person toward the self. The development of the self into full personhood can then never be posited as a project of self-development, aided and abetted by environment or technique. This radically qualifies all claims that parenting is a neutral process in the development of the self with respect to determining the actual content of the self.

However, this is a highly abstract and theoretical statement of the case. The material content of parenting is love given and experienced as openness of being in a structure of mutual interdependence. As Hans Urs von Balthasar writes, "No man reaches the core and ground of his own being, becoming free to himself and to all beings, unless love shines on him."[9] The creation of the original human person was an act of divine love, not merely of supernatural power. Supernatural power can create beasts, but not persons. Divine technology was shown to be insufficient in Genesis 2 when it came to "making" out of the dust a counterpart to the solitary male. Adam can be a creature through the power of divine fiat, but he can become a human person only through a process of differentiation, recognition, and response to another human self. Von Balthasar likens this creative act on God's part to that of a mother's love:

> God, who inclined toward his new-born creature with infinite personal love, in order to inspire him with it and to awaken the response to it in him, does in the divine supernatural order something similar to a mother. Out of the strength of her own heart she awakens love in her child in true creative activity.... The essential thing is, that the child, awakened thus to love, and already endowed by another's power of love, awakens also to himself and to his true freedom, which is in fact the freedom of loving transcendence of his narrow individuality.[10]

The failure of love at the level of cohumanity is consequently a deprivation of personhood, not merely an ethical fault. Likewise, a failure of love in response to God is a loss of personhood or, at the very least, a deformity of the self, not merely a religious fault. This is also why an unwillingness or a failure to love is already an act of violence against the person of another. This is surely what lies behind the teaching of Jesus in the Sermon on the Mount (Matt. 5) where hatred is already murder, lust is already adultery, and nonresistance to evil is a positive attack upon the humanity of others. Loving one's enemies is more than a tactic of nonresistance; it is the only creative act

---

9. Hans Urs von Balthasar, *A Theological Anthropology* (New York: Sheed and Ward, 1967), p. 87.
10. Ibid., p. 87.

possible when the social structure has itself become inhuman. The liberation of a recalcitrant child from the destructive stance of rebellion and disobedience cannot be done by appealing to the child itself. No single person can attain true freedom of personal being unless he or she experiences the openness of being on the part of another in the context of a social structure of coexistence.

Commenting on this same correlation of love between parent and child and subsequent capacity to love and trust others, Brigitte and Peter Berger say,

> Aristotle's famous view that if children did not love their parents and family members, they would love no one but themselves, is one of the most important statements ever made about the relation between family and society. The family permits an individual to develop love and security — and most important, the capacity to trust others. Such trust is the prerequisite for any larger social bonds. Only in the family are the individual's social tendencies aroused and developed and with these the capacity to take on responsibility for others. A person who has developed no family bonds will have a very hard time developing any larger loyalties in later life.[11]

The Bergers go on to say that an attack on the family structure in favor of democratic values that equalize the roles and relationships to a purely political or economic order is perverse and inherently destructive to personal life. The parenting role is not such that it can be delivered over to technicians or functionaries. We would say that this is because parenting is part of a developmental process by which "humanization" occurs, not merely socialization. And by *humanization* we mean the capacity to express those distinctives that reflect the divine image and likeness.

From this we conclude that the development of persons into some degree of maturity will be directly related to the actual demonstration of love within the primary social structure of each person's life. This is what we mean by *parenting*. Ordinarily, biological parents or adoptive parents form the primary social structure for this parenting to take place. However, as has been argued, parenting is never a neutral pedagogical activity. It will be either constructive or destructive, depending upon the degree to which openness of being is experienced as a positive force of interaction between the persons involved. In Judith Guest's novel *Ordinary People*, Beth Jarrett, an unfeeling mother, is unable to forgive or embrace her teenage son, Conrad, who has attempted suicide. The father's own ineffectual attempts to smooth over the situation only compound the problem, and he leaves the son to his own resources. Although he doesn't want to do so, Conrad seeks the assistance of a psychiatrist, and discovers a person sufficiently strong to confront pain within the

11. Berger and Berger, *The War Over the Family*, p. 174.

limits of love, and to give the necessary affirmation of love when it counted. As a result, in the end Conrad "parents" his own parents, by expressing his love for them out of the freedom of his own newly found personal being. This destroys the precarious balance that the mother has been attempting to maintain, and she leaves the family. However, it tips the father toward the son, in whose arms he begins to discover his own personhood.

But what do we make of the fact that the psychiatrist disappears from the scene precisely at the point where Conrad gains his own freedom to exercise personhood? If parenting is indispensable it also seems to be disposable. And what of our assertion that parenting is more than a technique by which one discovers one's own potentiality to be a person? If parenting is to some extent at least an ontological determinant of selfhood, what marks remain as evidence of the contribution of others to our own being? And what does it mean that the consequence of good parenting seems to entail the eventual freedom from dependence upon the one who parents?

These questions remind us that we must not invest the role of parenting with an indispensable status of its own. Parenting is somewhat like the "gift of the Spirit" to which Paul refers in his letter to the Corinthian church. The gift has no official status in terms of an office, but rather dissolves into the result that the gift produces. The "edification of the body" is the end of each gift of the Spirit. Likewise, the development of persons into individuals capable of receiving and giving love is the end of parenting. Psychotherapy is a professional form of intervention that picks up the parenting task in a clinical setting. We are not surprised that the relationship ends when the intervention is no longer necessary. In another setting, the psychotherapist and the client may also become friends who experience their cohumanity as part of an ongoing social unity. But this is not necessary in every case. The transition is more difficult with our biological parents. In this case, the consanguinity involved is expected to outlast the formal role of parenting, with the result that one's father or mother may also continue to be part of the enlarging network of loving community. Perhaps this is what the Psalmist David alluded to when he wrote, "But I have calmed and quieted my soul, like a child quieted [weaned] at its mother's breast; like a child that is quieted is my soul" (Ps. 131:2). The child who is weaned from the mother's breast may once again come within the mother's embrace, but with a freedom to be there without making insistent demands. The goal of parenting is freedom, which is itself the source of true love and community.

But what shall we say of the more difficult question concerning the "marks" that remain as evidence of the contribution of others? Do we actually imprint upon the being of those whom we parent some indelible personality characteristic that is unmistakably our own? If we do, then does this not appear to compromise the uniqueness and freedom of the other to become a person in his or her own right? And if we do not, then what does it mean to say that in parenting there is an ontological determination of the other so that becoming a person is a result of parenting?

These questions and the dilemma they pose result from the confusion of personality with personhood. To some extent our personality, as an acquired manifestation of behavioral patterns, may well be shaped or influenced by other "personalities" who have a strongly formative role in our development. However, what we mean by personhood is not identical with personality, though it does not exist apart from our own particular personality. When we become a person through the experiencing of love within responsible social structures, we become free to express our own unique and particular being in those relationships by means of and through our own personality. This is why a genuine meeting of the other person results in a knowledge of the other that can remain constant through an evolution of personality from one pattern to another. When personality changes result in loss of relationship, this is itself evidence that the relationship was only superficially related to personhood.

Perhaps one of the greatest tests of parenting is the capacity to allow significant development and change in personality without breaking contact with the person being parented. A professional therapist must learn how to do this if the therapy is to be effective. But this is not a matter of professional training; it is actually a matter of love. "Love bears all things, believes all things, hopes all things, endures all things," wrote the apostle Paul (1 Cor. 13:7). Love "takes hold" of the other person without letting go, and thus frees the other from all other determinations. Thus, love covers a multitude of sins (1 Pet. 4:8), casts out fear (1 John 4:18) and does no wrong to a neighbor (Rom. 13:10). The only mark left upon another person who becomes a free and whole person through parenting is the capacity to love. Because this mark is not an imprint of the personality of the one who parents in love, the significant link is the covenant that is remembered and kept. Not to forget one's parents but rather to honor them is both the responsibility and the joy of one who has become free through parenting. When Conrad Jarrett can finally say quietly to his father, "I love you," the love and friendship of the psychiatrist expressed through a professional role has left its mark.

THE ROLE OF PARENTS
IN PARENTING

We must now take up more specifically the role of parents in parenting. By *role* we mean a formative role, not a functional one. In particular, we will examine the purpose of parenting as well as its intended outcomes. We must be guided here by the basic assumption that parenting is a task that persons assume and fulfill in responsibility to a divine command. This places our discussion in a context that carries theological and biblical assumptions, which obviously, therefore, will bias our conclusions. From within the Judeo-Christian tradition, with guidelines set by the authority of Scripture, both Old and New Testaments, we seek to define the role of parenting in terms that are congruent with the most basic human task of becoming a person as well as with the divine mandate as to the origin and goal of human, personal existence.

The first aspect of the role of parenting is *to recognize and affirm the humanity of the child*. John Macmurray reminds us that the notion that children are subhuman until they are humanized through education and rational development is not only unbiblical but false:

> If the notion that children are little animals who acquire the characteristics of rational humanity through education, whose personalities are "formed" by the pressures brought to bear upon them as they grow up — if this notion seems to us simple common sense, and matter of everyday observation — it is because we share the traditional outlook and attitude of a culture which has been moulded by Greek and in particular by Aristotelian ideas. So much of common sense is the relic of past philosophies! Whatever its origin, this view is radically false.[12]

This notion, adds Macmurray, is not derived from empirical study of human persons, but is a priori and analogical. If it begins by empirical study of organic life, it betrays itself by making a logical move from organic to personal being. The study of persons, in particular of the mother/child relation, counters Macmurray, reveals an intrinsic personal and human capacity that belongs to infants and is not found in nonhuman offsprings.

The human infant, according to the Roman Catholic theologian Karl Rahner, possesses from the very beginning the value and depth of soul that characterizes the adult human. In his words, "The child is already the man."[13] It is not simply that the child has value because he has the potential of becoming a man, but because he already *is* that which the man, or the human adult, is. As the personal history of the child unfolds, he realizes and becomes what he already is. "The child is the man who is, right from the first, the partner of God." adds Rahner.[14]

The human infant, of course, does not know this. That is, the child cannot affirm this for itself from the beginning. Therefore, in addition to its physical

---

12. Macmurray, *Persons in Relation*, pp. 44-45.
13. Karl Rahner, "Ideas for a Theology of Childhood," in *Theological Investigations* (New York: Seabury Press, 1977), 8:37.
14. Ibid., p. 38.

weakness and vulnerability as creature, the child is especially vulnerable precisely because it is a *human* child. This vulnerability emerges as a need deeper than mere physical dependence. And it is this vulnerability that makes the contingency of human existence at its very inception a matter of both intense (and even tragic) concern as well as exquisite joy.

Yet it would be a mistake, Macmurray warns us, to assume that the inability of the child to express its own humanity in the form of personal self-recognition is a sign of the child's inability to communicate through response to a specific human act. From the significant other (the mother, in this case), the child derives the cognitive intentionality that keeps it alive. The infant does *know* that it has certain basic needs, and as such is motivated to express pain or discomfort, as well as pleasure when the need is met. Nonhuman creatures can express discomfort instinctually, says Macmurray, but this is not yet communication. Communication is the expression of unnecessary feelings, from the purely physical standpoint, which is a way of loving, and thus a way of knowing. This mutuality of interdependence between mother and child continues long past the point of pure physical dependence, and is coupled to the growing sense of self that the child experiences through parenting. Clara Mayo corroborates this from the field of social science:

> In man, this dependence of offspring is much longer than in animals and is guided by more than the biological heritage. Only sustained social contact enables the child to develop a sense of self and a capacity to cope with the tasks that the environment presents.[15]

The role of parenting in recognizing and affirming the humanity of the child takes place as the parent creates and sustains an environment in which physical actions are accompanied by personal actions, in which love is communicated through all of the "senses" by which the child is in contact with the parent. Not only is love communicated from parent to child, but the communication of the child with the parent is recognized, interpreted personally, and confirmed through response. These "nonverbal" communications are not precursors of later, more rational forms, but are themselves the very essence of rationality. For rationality, as John Macmurray has reminded us in another place, is the capacity to love objectively; that is, to relate in terms of the other.[16]

It can be helpful for us to see that childhood is not merely a stage in which a person moves to adulthood, or non-childhood. Rather, childhood is

---

15. Clara Mayo, "Man: Not Only an Individual, But a Member," *Zygon* 3 (March 1968): 21.
16. "The capacity to love objectively is the capacity which makes us persons. It is the ultimate source of our capacity to behave in terms of the object. It is the core of rationality." Macmurray, *Reason and Emotion* (London: Faber and Faber, 1935), p. 32.

itself a core of human life that endures as a quality of personal freedom and openness. It is, says Rahner, the original orientation to God, which, when fully matured in the adult, retains the original quality of childhood. For childhood is openness to being without guile. And the mature childhood of the adult, says Rahner, "is the attitude in which we bravely and trustfully maintain an infinite openness in all circumstances and despite the experiences of life which seem to invite us to close ourselves."[17]

In fulfilling the parenting role, adults must be able to bring their own adult childhood into being and participate with the child in the wonder and mystery of openness by which the original act of the self participates in a "knowing" relation to God. Religious education can never replace, nor seldom compensate for, the failure of parenting to affirm the child in its humanity by placing its sense of openness and wonder in touch with the reality of God. And God is love, and whoever abides in love abides in God (1 John 4:16).

A second aspect of the role of parenting is *to create and sustain the personal life of the child*. The physical act of procreation is not itself, of course, an act of creating human life — even nonhuman creatures bring forth their young in a similar manner. Therefore, in saying that parenting entails the responsibility to "create and sustain" personal life, we must immediately qualify that statement. Yet what we have earlier discussed as the responsibility to recognize and affirm the child as human forces upon us an active rather than passive role in the process of bringing forth and sustaining the life of a child. Allowing for the fact that the exact point in the physical process by which human life emerges cannot be determined with precision, parenting nonetheless actively undertakes the responsibility for protecting the physical existence of the child even before it leaves the mother's womb. Because the personal life of the child is dependent upon physical life, parenting actively prepares for the child's personal life by affirming and safeguarding its physical existence insofar as it is humanly possible. Theological anthropology does not confuse human life with physical, or mere creaturely, life. Therefore it avoids the stance of positing personal life in the form of rudimentary embryonic existence. It is not necessary to think of a fetus as a person in order to regard it as human. And because it must be regarded as human, it must be protected in its most vulnerable stage from being treated inhumanly. But that responsibility can be placed only under the role of parenting.

The development of personal individuality is a process of acquiring a "history" of the self.[18] Parenting creates and sustains personal life by reinforcing the child's own relationship with the external world in such a way that it

---

17. Rahner, "Ideas for a Theology of Childhood," p. 48.
18. Macmurray, *Persons in Relation*, p. 91.

achieves continuity and congruence. If, however, the child is confronted with the possibilities inherent in freedom too quickly and without preparation, the congruence of the self through a variety of experiences will be lost, and continuity will be secured only by a desperate clinging to a safe person or a predictable pattern. Continuity is important because it enables the person to maintain a consistent self-identity through a variety of circumstances and relationships. This is what we mean by the "history" of the self, by which self-identity is actually strengthened, not threatened, through experiencing change. Congruence, on the other hand, is the positive relation between the self and one's behavior at any given time. In other words, the self is integrated as an experiencing subject so that there is the maximum degree of unity between self-perception, action, and perception by others.[19] Obviously, continuity and congruity are quite closely connected, but each points to an essential aspect of the formation of personhood. Thus, a child "moves" through stages of development, each with a new set of behaviors and perceptions. But the core of self-identity is affirmed and sustained through the parenting process in such a way that the self grows toward increasing freedom in selecting the experiences and initiating behavior that is congruent with self-perception and in continuity with a history of the self.

There is a school of thought that holds that anxiety is the core experience of the self and the key to the existential life of the person, by which personhood or selfhood actually "comes into being."[20] However, parenting does not need to induce anxiety in a child in order to create the movement toward freedom. Anxiety is more the root of neurosis, which is nonhistorical being, than of creative personal life. It is the attendant phenomenon of experiencing threat to the continuity and congruence of personal existence. Of course it is always present to some degree or other. But it is not the core element in the self, nor can it be the source of creativity, for that would mean that the self is not really contingent upon love as the source of its own existence as a capacity to love, but actually contingent upon nonbeing.

From the perspective of a theological anthropology, the deepest and most fundamental urge or need in a child is the urge to experience belonging as a history of the self, as part of the story of life. This is why children are drawn so instantly and deeply into myth and storytelling. For the child, myth does not have the philosophical character of unreality or untruth, but instead becomes a kind of surrogate history of the self, which as yet has no depth of history. The storyteller, the child to whom the story is told, and the story

---

19. Ibid., p. 80.
20. This is Ernest Becker's thesis in *The Denial of Death* (New York: Macmillan, The Free Press, 1973).

itself merge into an event that fulfills the child's need to have a "story of one's own."

Successful parenting, then, results in the development of a child into an adult whose life is a story that can be told. That is, the child has become a person with a history (his or her story) and with the freedom to make history. The immature or underdeveloped person has little sense of personal history and little capacity to participate in history making. Rather, life becomes punctuated with a series of infatuations rather than love, compulsive spending of emotional resources rather than investment in a relation, and a trail of broken promises marked by "no forwarding address."

The role of parenting is to create a capacity for commitment that remains free from enslavement and is competent to experience the new without having to abandon the old. The test of parenting is not that the child never leaves home, but that when it does, it can always return, no matter what the conditions. And in returning, there is both something old and something new, to steal a phrase from the old wedding adage. Referring once again to Psalm 131:2 ("I have calmed and quieted my soul, like a child quieted [weaned] at its mother's breast"), we see that a literal rendering of the Hebrew pictures the child who has been weaned and has experienced the pain of withdrawal, now able to return to the mother's breast without compulsive need, but with remembrance of and new affirmation of belonging and love. There is a process of "weaning" that must take place in the development of a child into a mature adult. This is not a tearing away from one's history of belonging, but the beginning of one's own personal history, as well as the continuing of the history of the family. Where there is authentic family, there is a story!

We have outlined two aspects of the role of parenting in the development of persons: first, to recognize and affirm the humanity of the child, and second, to create and sustain the personal life of the child. We have already suggested that parenting seeks to develop the personal history of the child by introducing it to the world. We must now expand upon this as the third aspect of the role of parenting, which is *to contextualize and historicize the self as existing before and with God.*

We view the role of parenting as a responsibility that exists by virtue of the command of God. This is patently a theological assertion, and yet we do not think that it is an artificial or a contrived position. The command of God is not itself an arbitrary intrusion into an otherwise self-sufficient world. Rather, it is the positive determination by which human life comes into being, as well as the attendant providence by which it is sustained and oriented toward its true goal.

Theological anthropology has the courage to recognize the duality that intersects the core of the real world. Human existence is vulnerable on two counts. First, it is vulnerable because of its creatureliness, a necessary but insufficient condition of human life. It is the insufficiency of creatureliness itself that constitutes human life as fragile and vulnerable. Second, it is vulnerable because it emerges into an existence that is already historically conditioned by guilt and failure. Rahner reminds us eloquently of this fact:

> This history is, right from the outset, also a history of guilt, of gracelessness, of a refusal to respond to the call of the living God. The history of the guilt of mankind taken as an unity right from the beginning of that history regarded as a single whole is also a factor in the history of the individual. The love which brings grace to man, the love in which God himself with the fulness of his life gives himself to the individual is not simply, or in any obvious sense, an intrinsic element in a love which God might have borne right from the beginning towards a humanity which did not fall into sin. Rather it is a love which endures despite the fact that sin rose to power in history right at the origins of the human race.[21]

Parenting is necessary to place the child in that history which will call him or her to responsibility for that history; to enable the child to "lose its innocence" and so understand, and not deny, its own propensity for evil. It is only sentimental idealism that pretends to the child that it is innocent. This is a denial of the child's own history and its solidarity with the history of the whole human race.

However, we must say immediately that the contextualizing of the self through the role of parenting is done before and with God. Therefore, the experience of grace is prior to and fundamental for the experience of the self under judgment. It is the responsibility of those who parent children to create the context by which all human existence is brought under grace, and therefore under judgment and hope. This is what it means to say that parenting is accountable to the commandment of God rather than to intrinsic human or creaturely possibilities. Parenting can only be saved from its own destructive idealism and self-serving motivations by taking place as a context in which God's own history with humanity is authentically portrayed.

Parenthood is not a form of "limitless love," to use Miller's apt phrase, by which he exposed the fallacy of presumed innocence in his play *After the Fall*. When Quentin set out to "save" a prodigal young woman by marrying her and attempting to stay with her even through her own self-destructive impulses, he discovered in his own attempt at "parenting" a failure to take into account his own lack of innocence:

---

21. Rahner, "Ideas for a Theology of Childhood," p. 39.

God's power is love without limit. But when a man dares reach for that ... he is only reaching for the power. Whoever goes to save another person with the lie of limitless love throws a shadow on the face of God.

Who can be innocent again on this mountain of skulls? ... and what's the cure? Or is that why she hopes, because she knows? What burning cities taught her and the death of love taught me; that we are very dangerous! ... Is the knowing all? To know, and even happily, that we meet unblessed; not in some garden of wax fruit and painted leaves, that lie of Eden, but after, after the Fall, after many, many deaths.[22]

What is theologically known as "original sin" has an existential reality in the personal existence of the child becoming an adult. Without parenting that attempts to contextualize the self in historical responsibility for sin, the child has no way of dealing with its own destructive impulses. If these are minimized as mere "bad" or "unruly" behavior that training will overcome, the destructive actions and attitudes become associated with impersonal or, even worse, demonic powers that are alien to the self. At best, such alien and impersonal movements within the self are repressed and denied, leading to a perfectionist and compulsively "moral" personality, which is both psychologically and spiritually unhealthy.

Because the child is essentially a person, deviations and distortions must be dealt with as personal. This is the role of parenting; the creation of an environment that brings all actions of persons into accountability to others is both liberating and reconciling. A child must become responsible for its own evil (destructive tendencies) and for the other's good. Responsible existence in cohumanity with openness to the presence of God at the boundaries of the self is the basis for what is called moral character.

The biblical ethic, accordingly, is subsumed under the act of love as responsible personhood. "Owe no one anything, except to love one another," wrote the apostle Paul, "for he who loves his neighbor has fulfilled the law. . . . Love does no wrong to a neighbor; therefore love is the fulfilling of the law" (Rom. 13:8, 10). God's history with humanity, which culminated in the person of Jesus Christ, radically challenged and overcame the tendency to isolate evil in demonic powers over persons and to isolate goodness in self-righteous legal morality at the expense of the "sinner." The kingdom of God creates a new community out of the old by first of all affirming the love of God for human persons in the actual state and condition in which they are found. However,

---

22. Arthur Miller, *After the Fall* (Middlesex, England: Penguin Books, 1968), pp. 113, 119.

self-destructive and negating actions of personal existence are now contextualized as a form of rebellion against God, who manifests himself in personal actions and relations. Thus, what had become impersonal, both evil and goodness, now becomes highly personal. This is the source of liberation from bondage and the source of true healing and wholeness.

The project of the self is not to maintain innocence as a desperate attempt to survive under the terrible and impersonal mandate of law, but to take account of one's own destructive tendencies by participating in the personal good of community. Responsibility for the formation of community and the upholding of community in the face of the centrifugal force of self-will is itself an ethical action. It is the positive action of one who is not "innocent" of hateful and hurtful attitudes and actions. When parenting refuses to grant the freedom for a child to take responsibility for its own destructive (evil) actions within the responsibility for participating in the formation of family, the child is forced to present a behavior of goodness, while at the same time forced to deny personal accountability for wrong or destructive actions. Religious education as well as education in moral values can never replace and seldom, if ever, compensate for the lack of parenting by which personal accountability for one's own evil and another's good is not developed as a core of self-awareness.

In every hour the human race continues, we can now say. But it is more than a race for survival of the fittest. The role of parenting is to slow the race to a walk, and to learn to tell a story along the way. Growing up is really child's play

CHAPTER SIX

THE ROLE OF PARENTING
IN THE DEVELOPMENT
OF PERSONS

I often begin one of my lectures to my students with the statement, "I believe that there is no such thing as an 'individual,' only members." The response is predictable. The notion of individualism runs so deep in our culture that for anyone to challenge it is next to apostasy. At the heart of my point, however, is an issue that is important to our discussion in this chapter. The term *individual* has been expanded to such an extent that it no longer is useful when thinking and talking about the family because the family is only one of many groups in which the person has membership. In this sense of the term *member* the human person is a collage of memberships that often have competing demands and seemingly legitimate expectations of the person. A focus upon the "individual" is reductionistic in the baldest Newtonian terms and misses completely the systemic nature of human persons.

It is within this context that two statements by Carl Whitaker of the University of Wisconsin take on significance. The first is that whoever human persons are, they are "only fragments of families." The second is his famous definition of a wedding: "A wedding is two families sending forth a scapegoat, each hoping to reproduce itself." What Whitaker illustrates that is of importance to our discussion is an emphasis upon the sense of the collectivity that exists within a family and the insistence that such attachments, or sentiments, are the products of a heritage or history of the family in combination with the forces of today. To neglect either the heritage of the family or the network of relationships that constitute the family system in the here and now is to distort the true and essential meaning of the person.

Thus, according to this approach, "family" becomes the essential unit of interaction within the world of the human person and hence the central unit of society. Taking this a step further, we can say that of all the relationships that exist within the family, the central, most important relationship is the parent/child relationship—however much we might want to hold marriage up to be the single most important relationship. Further, the thesis of this chapter is that parenting is the most critical skill of the family. It is the ability or inability of the natural parents or parental surrogates to fulfill their parenting function that establishes the capacity of the human person to be functional or dysfunctional both as a person and as a functioning member in his or her own newly formed family of procreation. Behind every marriage lies the early parenting experiences and relationships of the partners.[1]

It is useful at this point to cast into historical context the question of what should be the first, necessary focus for a theology of the family. Do we begin with marriage (Brunner) or with the parent/child relationship (Barth)? The church often is the handmaiden of the dominant culture, unfortunately even when that culture is decidedly ascriptural. Christopher Lasch has added a helpful discussion in which he traced the emergence of the contemporary emphasis upon "companionship" and hence the emphasis upon marriage.[2] The family, once studied as an "institution," is now studied as a "source of affective stimuli" for better or for worse. According to Lasch, after World War I, sociology as a discipline sought to explain the forces at work in the Industrial Revolution. The "Chicago School" became the center of scholarly debate as it explicated a "sociology of urbanization." Urban sociology came to dominate the perceptions and interpretations of society. At the core of this urban sociology, with regard to the family, was the doctrine of the "transfer of functions." This theory posited the belief that as society increased in complexity, velocity, transcience, and mobility, the family, especially the patriarchal family, ceased to be able to adapt effectively. What resulted was the takeover of critical functions by other institutions. The "institutional" functions of the family declined and the "personality" functions took on greater importance.

In 1938 William F. Ogburn posited seven functions that prior to modern times provided the family with its power and prestige.[3] Those functions were economic, status-giving, educational, religious, recreational, protective, and affectional. The procreative function was subsumed under the affectional function. According to Ogburn,

> The dilemma of the modern family is caused by the loss of many of these functions in recent times. The economic function has gone to the factory, store, office, and restaurant, leaving little of economic

---

1. In fact, my twenty-plus years as a therapist have convinced me that our choice of marital partners is usually an unconscious choice either to recreate our earlier parenting relationships or to repair the felt damage that was done. Either way, the choice of a marriage partner is rarely a random selection. For an excellent discussion of this issue see David Klimek, *Beneath Mate Selection and Marriage* (New York: Van Nostrand Reinhold, 1979).

2. Christopher Lasch, *Haven in a Heartless World* (New York: Basic Books, 1977).

3. W. F. Ogburn, "The Changing Functions of the Family," *The Family* 19 (1938): 139-43.

activity to the family of the city apartment. About half of education has been transferred to the schools, where the teacher is a part-time or substitute parent. Recreation is found in moving pictures, parks, city streets, clubs, with bridge and radio at home. Religion doesn't seem to make as much difference in family matters as formerly, grace at meals and family prayers are rare. As to protection, the child is protected at home, but the state helps also with its child labor laws and reform schools. The police and social legislation indicate how the protective function has been transferred to the state, as has the educational function. Family status has been lost in marked degree along with these other functions in an age of mobility and large cities. It is the individual that has become more important and the family less so. On the other hand the family still remains the center of the affectional life and is the only recognized place for producing children.

From this survey it may seem that at least six of the seven functions have been reduced as family activities in recent times, and it may be claimed that only one remains as vigorous and extensive as in prior eras.[4]

Thus the emotional services the family performed became the critical issue and the companionate model of marriage, the arch-type of the affectional function, became essential. This "indispensability of the emotional services it performed, simultaneously justified the transfer of the family's functions to other agencies. Sociologists assumed, in fact, that urbanization made such a 'transfer of functions' inevitable."[5]

The next step, according to Lasch, was to actualize the affectional function. "Friendship" rather than loyalty, responsibility, or even "love" became an integrating theme. The child, in order to perform well within its world, needed wider and broader opportunities for affiliation. So did marriage partners. The end result (to collapse several chapters into a single sentence), became the "nonbinding commitment" of Open Marriage, the open-ended opportunity to experience as many positive affective relationships as is possible. Lasch's summary of the issue is especially pointed:

> The fear and rejection of parenthood, the tendency to view the family as nothing more than marriage, and the perception of marriage as merely one in a series of nonbinding commitments, reflect a growing distrust of the future and a reluctance to make provisions for it — to lay up goods and experience for the use of the next generation.[6]

It is this "distrust of the future and the reluctance to make provisions for it" that has led us to posit the parent/child relationship rather than marriage as the necessary "beginning" for a theology of the family.

---

4. Ibid.
5. Lasch, *Haven in a Heartless World*, p. 37.
6. Ibid., p. 139.

In his determination to construct a "holy history" and to be in fellowship with humanity, God created man as male and female, that is, as cohumanity. Man was created as social, personal, sexual, and spiritual — and as such in the "image and likeness of God." But sin marred that creation and God, acting in grace through his Word, began a program to reconcile humankind to himself. But what enables us to "know" this? God typically acts through intermediaries — in particular through his living Word, Jesus. The mediatorial paradigm in Hebrews 4 explains that, because of the fullness of his humanity, Jesus is able to sympathize with us, to understand our weaknesses, to extend both mercy and grace to us in time of need. Hebrews 4 delineated the Godward side of the reconciliation equation, but what about the manward side? What is it that allows man to be able to "hear"? From whom does he learn to receive sympathy, understanding, mercy, and grace? These "human" capacities are not innate. They are not genetically coded into the human infant at conception. Rather, they are learned. The potential of all that is human, all that is social, personal, sexual, and spiritual comes alive first of all and best of all in the first "I/Thou" relationship experienced by the infant, the parent/child relation. It is the parenting process that first transmits both the experience and knowledge of reconciliation — effectively or ineffectively. Like the process of therapy, in which the therapist engages in a kind of reparenting, the parent engages in a kind of re-creation of the *imago Dei*. This is not to say that the child is "born again" simply in being parented. It is only meant to say that the natural or surrogate parent provides the ecological reality in which the child learns his or her humanity. The parent provides the child with the opportunity to grow "in wisdom and in stature, and in favor with God and man" (Luke 2:52).

The parent also provides the child with a model of the parenting process so that in years to come when the child has become a parent, the eschatological baton can be passed from generation to generation.

> When your son asks you in time to come, "What is the meaning of the testimonies and the statutes and the ordinances which the Lord our God has commanded you?" then you shall say to your son . . . (Deut. 6:20)

The "meaning" of the word of reconciliation is embodied in the ecological reality of the parent/child relationship. The capacity to both "know" and "experience" is necessary to complete the reconciliation equation.

We begin, therefore, with the parent/child relationship because it is within that relationship that the process of socialization, the dynamic of parenting, begins. And it is to the literature in this field that we turn in order to better understand the processes that transpire between parent and child.

SOCIALIZATION:
THE PROCESS BETWEEN
PARENT AND CHILD

Students of socialization ask the question, "How is it possible for a society to endure and to continue to develop?"[7] According to Orville Brim, socialization is that process "by which persons acquire the knowledge, skill, and dispositions to make them more or less able members of their society."[8] It is the function of socialization to transform the human raw material of society into good working members. Through the process of socialization the past becomes the future, the parent becomes "Thou" to the child's "I" and vice versa. The products of socialization (i.e., values, beliefs, attitudes, roles, and norms) are developed through the natural dependencies of the child, that is, its need for care and information.[9] The child either does or doesn't "learn" to know God, to become fully human, to be differentiated as male or female. For every person someone or something stands in the parenting role and begins the re-creation of the *imago Dei*. Unfortunately, that process fails miserably for many. For others it works relatively well. Probably more forcefully than we would like to admit, the grace of God is conditioned by that process. By *conditioned* we simply mean that his grace is either facilitated or frustrated by the parenting process as it is mediated to the person. Part of the human condition is freedom — and part of that freedom is as parent to participate in or hinder the grace of God from generation to generation.

At this point a recapitulation might be helpful. First of all, we have affirmed the importance of the parent/child relationship in the formation of a theology of the family. Second, we have suggested that much of the insistence and interest upon the marriage relationship as primary stems not so much from a theological necessity as from the influence of contemporary culture with its erosion of the family as institution and the subsequent emphasis upon marriage as a depository of nonbinding commitments, with the affectional function held out to be all-important. Third, we have suggested that Jesus Christ in his mediatorial function made God fully "knowable" but that it yet remains necessary for the child through the parent/child interaction to learn "how to know." If the Word has "spoken," the human person must still be taught "to hear." And fourth, we have suggested that the teaching of the child "to know and to hear" God is accomplished through the process of socialization: of inculcating the values, beliefs, attitudes, roles, and norms associated with

---

7. Orville Brim and Stanton Wheeler. *Socialization After Childhood* (New York: John Wiley and Sons, 1966), p. 4.

8. Ibid., p. 3.

9. Cf. E. Jones and H. B. Girard. *Foundations of Social Psychology* (New York: John Wiley and Sons, 1967), pp. 75-156.

the stream of holy history; a process within each generation in which the reconciliation equation is repeated and made complete. God always has his witness in each and every generation. A significant dimension of that witness involves the "older" transmitting the knowledge of God, his mercy and his grace in Jesus Christ to the "younger" so that when they ask "What do these things mean?" they have their answer.

THE TASKS OF PARENTING

Last of all we move beyond the processes of socialization in an attempt to elaborate the parenting role in more detail. This is not to imply that socialization is an all-inclusive term nor that the following is all-inclusive. What I would like to suggest is a fivefold developmental process that follows the parenting theories of writers such as Bowlby, Erikson, and the object-relation theorists Klien and Horner.[10]

The first task of the parent is *the task of attachment.* Because the human infant is absolutely dependent, the role of care-giver is primary. The studies by Harlow and Spitz and the psychology of Bowlby are useful in describing the kinds of anxiety an infant experiences in the first few months of life and the infant's critical need physically and psychologically at this point. It is through the attachment process that the natural anxiety of affect dependence is mediated, trust is engendered, and the basic self begins to emerge. The initial position of the infant, however, is one in which the self is in the dependent position. It is wholly at the mercy of the primary care-giver. At no other time is the human more vulnerable. There are no defenses. There is no ability to care for one's self. The totality of the emerging person's self is defined by the responses of their "first love," that is, their primary care-giver, usually the mother. If the relationship is warm, nurturing, and infused with joy, the infant develops the basic and necessary ability to trust, founded upon the certain and predictable responses of the care-giver. If, on the other hand, that care is thwarted by circumstances, ambivalence, or by the dysfunction of the care-giver's ability to relate unconditionally to the infant, a state of mistrust is generated and the consequences are life-long.

The second task of parenting is *the task of differentiation.* Very early in the first year the infant begins to realize that he or she is not joined to the mother. When she leaves the room the infant is left behind. When the infant cries because of pain or discomfort the mother doesn't always respond im-

---

10. See John Bowlby, *Attachment* (New York: Basic Books, 1969); Erik Erikson, *Childhood and Society* (New York: Norton and Co., 1960); Althea J. Horner, *Object Relations and the Developing Ego in Therapy* (New York: Jason Aronson, 1979).

mediately. Other objects in the infant's world begin to take on significance, whether they are stuffed animals, hanging mobiles, or parenting alternatives such as the father. The task of the primary care-giver at this stage is to encourage the infant to expand his or her world to include other sources of meaningful stimuli and to avoid the extremes of limiting the infant to the world of the mother or of abandoning the infant to the multiplicity of outside care-givers who may or may not create a reliable nurturing world for the infant.

This stage of differentiation is later played out in bold relief in the adolescent years, when the infant — now grown to be a young person — must be released from the bonds of the parental family. If the earlier process of differentiation operated at either of the extremes, the parental experience with the emerging adolescent takes on an overly centrifugal or expelling character or an overly centripetal or binding character. The seeds for the parent/adolescent experience are sown in the quality of relationship between the infant and the primary care-giver.

The third task is *the task of separation and individuation.* Healthy parents raise their children not to need them. They work themselves out of a job. Unfortunately, many parents begin this task far later than is necessary. Although it begins as early as ten months with the infant's growing skills (such as learning to walk by itself), the task itself is stretched out over the very early years. "Me do it" is the bane of every parent during these months of the child's early life. What is at stake is the child's sense of mastery of its world apart from the mother, and the freedom to fail if necessary and to know that its failures will not end in catastrophic loss or disaster. At this stage the parent(s) are faced with the delicate balance between the child's independence and autonomy and its dependence upon the parent.

Latent within this stage and the task of separation and individuation is the issue referred to in the literature as "rapprochment."[11] This term is defined as the natural ambivalence experienced by the child when it begins to realize the implications of its growing independence and autonomy. If the child gets too good at it, it will not need its mother. Often during these months or years there is an upsurge in separation anxiety, in which the child backs away from its emerging independence and experiences a normal time of anxiety or clinging to the mother. What the child needs is the reassurance of the care-giver that her presence and support can be depended upon and that as the child ventures out into the world the care-giver will be a steady source of support and encouragement. The message must be "You can't go wrong if you grow up. It's OK not to need me. I'm with you even if I don't do things for you."

The fourth task of parenting is *the task of establishing constancy.* This

---

11. Horner, *Object Relations and the Developing Ego,* p. 33.

task is predicated upon the successful completion of the first three. It has to do with the final outfitting of the self in the child so that it is able to tolerate the natural ambivalences of relationships and the ambiguities of life. Anna Freud wrote that this stage of constancy is the ability "to retain attachment even when the person is unsatisfying."[12] If the primary care-giver has been basically dependable, nurturing, and loving, and has been able to release the child to become a self of its own, the next stage for the child is to realize that the mother, or anyone else in fact, cannot be there always and in every way. The child learns to depend upon itself at all times, and to forgive either itself or others when appropriate. No one can be perfect, and to demand perfection of oneself or of others is unrealistic. Constancy implies the attribution of permanence and trust even when the immediate results suggest otherwise.

The fifth task of parenting is *the task of generalization*. During this time the child recognizes its interdependence upon others. This is when the position of the self becomes "I/thou." It is the position of the prodigal son returning to his father. It is the dialogue between the self and the other in which the person declares "I am responsible to and for you as well as for myself." It is the position of emerging community; of mutual interdependence — the position in which the "one another" imperatives of the New Testament become relevant. It is the position in which the law of Christ is being fulfilled.

CONCLUSION

In terms of parenting, these five tasks are developmental, each necessary for those that follow. Thus, the absolute dependency of the person as infant is secured through the process of attachment to the dependable care-giver. The self begins to emerge in an environment of acceptance and joy. Next, the infant begins to differentiate itself from its care-giver and to develop a sense of its own self as distinct from others. Having become aware of its growing sense of differentiation, the infant/toddler enters into the journey toward separation and individuation even in the midst of rapprochment or self-doubt. From the resolution of this doubt comes the quality of constancy or the ability to trust and to forgive both self and others. And last of all comes the stage of generalization or healthy interdependence in which the child begins to recognize its responsibility not only for itself but also for the welfare of others.

What I am suggesting here is that these necessary tasks are foundational to the biblical injunction to leave one's father and mother and to cleave to one's spouse. Whether that leaving involves the commitment to marriage or

---

12. Anna Freud, "Remarks in a Panel Discussion," *International Journal of Psycho-Analysis* 49:506-7.

the commitment to others in community, the process is not complete until mutual interdependence is effected.

Parenting, therefore, is the arena in which the human person learns the necessary skills to function as an adult — whether married or single. In that sense and for that reason we begin with parenting in our developmental model.

PART FOUR

MARRIAGE AS AN EXPRESSION OF LOVE AND SEXUALITY

CHAPTER SEVEN

BONDING WITHOUT BONDAGE

"**O**NE ought to marry at all costs," Plato reportedly advised, "for if it proves to be a happy relationship, one will experience bliss and heavenly delight. If it proves to be an unhappy relationship, one may then become a philosopher, and experience the joys of the mind."

The fact that this quotation betrays a certain cynicism concerning the estate of marriage only shows that there is nothing new under the sun. And yet, if contemporary sociologists and psychologists are accurate in their assessment, marriage and human sexuality together constitute the greatest crisis for modern society. We may generally anticipate that roughly one-third of all marriages contracted in any given year in the United States will end in divorce — and in certain sections of the country, the ratio is one out of two. For several years, Los Angeles County has granted more divorce decrees than the number of marriage licenses issued. There can be little doubt that the critical problem underlying the general malaise of family life in North America is the instability and unhealthiness of marriage as a social unit. It is further postulated that this dis-ease in the state of marriage is a symptom of a more fundamental confusion of human sexuality, linked with a basic incompetence in developing and sustaining mature covenant relationships.

I do not intend in this chapter to set forth a basic theology of sexuality, nor will I review and critically analyze the literature on sexuality and marriage.[1] My concern is more limited: it focuses upon the specific nature of

---

1. For a theology of sexuality, see Ray S. Anderson, *On Being Human* (Grand Rapids: Eerdmans, 1982), chap. 8. For a review of the literature on a theology of marriage, see Dwight H. Small, *Christian: Celebrate Your Sexuality* (Old Tappan, NJ: Revell, 1974). Small provides a helpful source for bibliographic research in his critical notes, as well as a competent analysis of major theological perspectives on sexuality and marriage. For a recent discussion of a theology of sexuality focusing on current issues in male and female relationships, see Lisa Sowle Cahill, *Between the Sexes: Foundations for a Christian Ethics of Sexuality* (Philadelphia: Fortress Press, 1985). The approach and literature cited in this book take note of recent discussion in Roman Catholic theology. Gilbert Bilezikian, Professor of Biblical Studies at Wheaton College, has contributed a scholarly and helpful book on male and female sex roles from a biblical perspective, *Beyond Sex Roles: a Guide for the Study of Female Roles in*

marriage with respect to the basic encounter of male and female in covenant partnership as set forth in the preceding chapters. We have attempted to present a developmental model by which persons experience their own human selfhood as cohumanity, and by which they develop competence in creating and sustaining covenant-partner relations. While we have established the concept of covenant as the basic paradigm of family, we have not as yet delineated the basic structure of family itself. In now taking up this task, our first step will be to look at marriage as it stands independent of family as a sociological entity, and yet as the theological and practical sources of family. We ought not to consider marriage a component of a general concept of family. Rather, understood theologically, marriage stands as the concrete foundation of family.[2] Consequently, our task is to set forth a theological and critical basis for understanding the nature of marriage as an expression of human love and sexuality. Coupled with this theological endeavor will be certain pastoral perspectives — for our aim is not merely to view marriage theoretically, but to provide a basis for preventing marital breakdowns as well as for healing and renewal where the breakdown has occurred.

MARRIAGE AS
A COVENANT PARTNERSHIP

At the outset, we must also make clear a subtle but important distinction between a theological and an ethical view of marriage. Emil Brunner asserts that marriage, in the full sense of the word, represents an ethical solution to the problem of the relation between the sexes.[3] In his view, the erotic sexual impulse, basically created as good, has become, through sin, the greatest danger for the individual as well as for society. Thus, he posits marriage as the only optimum containment for this otherwise unbridled impulse.[4] Sexuality, argues Brunner, is sanctified only through marriage, unless one chooses total abstinence. But abstinence is essentially a negative means of ethical life. And Brunner believes that the sexual drive under the power of sin is not likely to be controlled successfully, because it is basically an "unnatural" form of human existence. Dwight Small agrees in essence with Brunner when he argues that

---

the Bible (Grand Rapids: Baker, 1985). Bilezikian examines the major biblical texts that relate to these issues from the perspective of a biblical theology that emphasizes the redemptive role of Christ in restoring the basic equality of male and female sex roles in the family and in the church. The extensive bibliography will be of help to many, as will the copious critical notes interacting with many current publications.

2. Cf. Karl Barth, who says that marriage is not subordinate to family, but family is subordinate to marriage (CD III/4, p. 189).

3. Emil Brunner, Love and Marriage (London: Collins, Fontana, 1970), p. 183.

4. Ibid., p. 195.

a "theology of sexuality is the sexuality of marriage in its fullest definition."[5] Interestingly, both Brunner and Small reject Barth's claim that human sexuality is a determination of human existence as the image and likeness of God and thus exists prior to and independent of marriage as a true order.

We can contrast Brunner's ethical view of marriage with Barth's more theological view. The question of the sexual implications of cohumanity as male and female does not coincide with the question of marriage, argues Barth.[6] In other words, "the ethical question in relation to the sphere of male and female cannot be exhaustively discussed in the problem of marriage."[7] Whereas for Brunner sexuality is sanctified as an ethical existence under the command of God only in the marriage relation, for Barth, the command of God "sanctifies man by including his sexuality within his humanity, and challenging him even in his bodily nature and therefore in his sexual life, in his answering of the problem of sex relationship, to be true man."[8] The sexual relation of man and woman has already been constituted a true order of humanity, says Barth, as an integral part of total humanity as male and female. Marriage, as an exemplification of the total encounter of male and female in covenant partnership, thus integrates sexuality into total humanity.

We do not mean to caricature the positions of Barth and Brunner to make it appear that they are further apart than they actually are. The difference is subtle because both advocate monogamy as the sole form of physical sexual expression under the command of God. And yet the difference between a theological view of marriage and sexuality and an ethical view is important. Brunner does posit a basic I-Thou relation as intrinsic to the image of God. But because he rejects the notion that this also includes sexuality as male and female, he must of necessity introduce marriage into the discussion of sexuality as the ethical presupposition of a sexual self-understanding as man and woman. This, it seems, has serious consequences for understanding the role of sexuality in the case of the unmarried person as well as for a discussion of the matter of homosexuality. If, as Small argues (following Brunner), the marital pair is the basic model of man and woman as a community of love and all other relations are peripheral to it, then marriage will be offered as the highest — if not the only — possibility for authentic humanity.[9]

On the other hand, following Barth, humanity as determined by God is *co*humanity, existing concretely as either male or female. Marriage, then, is not the only ethical justification of sexuality understood as authentic male and

---

5. Small, *Christian: Celebrate*, p. 221n.29.
6. *CD* III/4, p. 118.
7. Ibid., p. 140.
8. Ibid., p. 132.
9. Small, *Christian: Celebrate*, p. 137.

female humanity, even though it alone offers the only partnership in which sexual relation has its intended consummation and completion. This decentralizes the view that marriage is the only context in which male and female sexuality can be discussed ethically. Thus, sexuality is liberated from the need to be denied or repressed. The command of God, says Barth, requires no "liberation from sex" as a negative ethical act.[10] Marriage is not seen as a "containment" of that which has no other ethical point of reference, but as the "contextualizing" of that which comes to expression in the total encounter of man and woman. "Coitus without co-existence is demonic," says Barth—within as well as outside marriage.[11] Because sexuality is set within the command of God in terms of authentic humanity, marriage does not constitute the basis for a sexual ethic, but itself comes under the true order of sexuality as cohumanity. Marriage, as encounter between man and woman, rather than constituting a sanctification of "unbridled sexuality," is sanctified in the command of God that relates sexuality to coexistence as personal humanity.

We shall have more to say about what it means that marriage takes place under the "command of God," but for now it must also be said that this divine command does not take place independent of the human act of response and recognition. While marriage is more than love, it involves the mutual recognition, choice, and commitment of two people in covenant partnership. God joins together actually as well as theoretically. He joins together in and by the encounter and decision of the two who form the union; not only on the basis of this human act of love but coincidental with it and as its objective validation. What begins as affection and feelings of love, says Brunner, is absorbed into personal will expressed as commitment in marriage.

According to Barth, love, in contradistinction to mere affection,

> may be recognised by the fact that it is determined, and indeed determined upon the life-partnership of marriage. Love does not question; it gives an answer. Love does not think; it knows. Love does not hesitate; it acts. Love does not fall into raptures; it is ready to undertake responsibilities. Love puts behind it all the Ifs and Buts, all the conditions, reservations, obscurities and uncertainties that may arise between a man and a woman. Love is not only affinity and attraction; it is union. Love makes these two persons indispensable to each other.[12]

Even if the entrance into marriage is superficial, even if it is virtually a blunder, continues Barth, what was not marriage can later become marriage.[13] This is

---

10. *CD* III/4, pp. 131-32.
11. Ibid., p. 133.
12. Ibid., p. 221.
13. Ibid., p. 215.

so because fidelity awakens love as the result of a relationship that honors coexistence as a concrete manifestation of the divine command. Fidelity, then, is the human source of stability and permanence in marriage. The positive expression of will to partnership, fidelity can reawaken a love that barely exists or has even died.

But fidelity is more than a commitment to the other person based upon feelings of love. If it is only that, love's failure to sustain its own cause when it is not reciprocated will undermine it. Fidelity is the surrender of one's own cause to the cause of the other. Coexistence then becomes a partnership in which the particularity of the other becomes an irrevocable source of one's own destiny.

Hidden in this particularity is the origin of the concept of monogomy. Despite the fact that one can love more than one person at a time — for love itself is not the only source of fidelity — one can experience the exclusivity of the divine command with only one other. Inevitably we become confused when we base the principle of monogamous marriage on the notion of the exclusivity of love. This is where Brunner failed in his argument for monogamy. He asserts that natural love is in its essence monogamous, despite the tendencies toward polygamy expressed in various cultures.[14] Barth rightly argues that Brunner's notions are based on human experience rather than on divine command.[15] "It is God's election and covenant, says Barth, "which gives unconditional and compelling character to the requirement of monogamy. . . . In His election and His covenant it is not merely the electing divine Partner who is utterly one, . . . the creaturely and elected partner . . . is always singular as well.[16] Despite the tendentious theological argument that Barth uses to make his case, it remains compelling precisely because the divine determination of cohumanity is concretely and particularly male and female. Even at the level of physical sexuality, complementarity is essentially a polarity between two. Thus, though one can love more than one person simultaneously in terms of general human encounter, one cannot be bound in a relationship of fidelity to more than one at the same time. And the singularity of sexual union expresses this quite particularly.

Having said all this, are we tempted to respond with the disciples, "If such is the case of a man with his wife, it is not expedient to marry" (Matt. 19:10)? We hope not. While we have set marriage within the absolute determination of a divine command, we have not set it above the reality and practice of human existence. Those who seek to enter into marriage ought to be counseled to consider it seriously, but also to view it realistically, not ideally. Marriage

---

14. Brunner, *Love and Marriage*, p. 189.
15. *CD* III/4, pp. 200-211.
16. Ibid., p. 198.

can never be the solution to problems of personal unhappiness or loneliness. It can never be the relational horizon within which one expects to meet all his or her personal needs. Marriage offers an expression of love and sexuality not realizable in any other human relationship, but it is no more human than any other human task or relationship. And in particular, because marriage takes place under the divine command,

> the sphere of the relationships of man and woman as they are embodied and lived out among us human beings is not simply a labyrinth of errors and failings, a morass of impurity, or a vale of tears at disorder and distress. For by the grace of God ... there are always in this sphere individual means of conservation and rescue, of deliverance and restoration, assured points and lines even where everything seems to vacillate and dissolve, elements of order in the midst of disorder.... And if there is no perfect marriage, there are marriages which for all their imperfection can be and are maintained and carried through, and in the last resort not without promise and joyfulness, arising with a certain necessity, and fragmentarily, at least, undertaken in all sincerity as a work of free life-fellowship. There is also loyalty even in the midst of disloyalty and constancy amid open inconstancy.... Thus even where man does not keep the command, the command keeps man.... He who here commands does not only judge and forgive; He also helps and heals.[17]

Is marriage, then, a social contract that can be broken when one or both of the contracting parties violate the contract, or is it a covenant partnership that, once entered into, can never be dissolved? Well, it is both. While a social contract based upon mutual conditions of good will and reciprocity does not contain within it the quintessential aspect of covenant love, covenant love can come to expression through a social contract. It is our opinion that all humans can express a dimension of covenant love because they are created in the divine image and likeness. But God is the source of covenant love, which he expressed through his actions of bonding with Israel and then with all humanity through Jesus Christ. From the human perspective, the essence of a marriage is the social contract explicitly grounded in a relation of human sexuality, male and female, which finds its implicit source of covenant love in God's own commandment and gift of love.

MARRIAGE AS
SEXUAL PARTNERSHIP

The relationship of human sexuality to marriage is a matter of particular concern and often of confusion. Marriage counselors tell us that most marital

---

17. Ibid., pp. 239-40.

problems include some dimension of incompatibility or dysfunction at the level of sexual relationship. We are reminded here of Barth's warning: "coitus without co-existence is demonic."

But there is even more confusion in the so-called "premarital" experience of sexual relation. Does sexual relation itself constitute marriage in God's eyes? If so, then what does "premarital" mean in terms of the sexual relation? Sexual intercourse between man and woman is presupposed by the command of God by which human existence is set within a divine order. To be human is not only to be male or female, but to be male *and* female. Not only does God determine us to be either male or female, but also that we are to be male with respect to the female, and female with respect to the male. This reminds us of Paul's teaching that "in the Lord woman is not independent of man nor man of woman; for as woman was made from man, so man is now born of woman" (1 Cor. 11:11-12). Coexistence is the mutual recognition of the determination of one for the other and one with the other. To relate in such a way that this determination does not result in coexistence is a fundamental disorder, what Barth calls "demonic." That which stands in defiance of the command of God has its source in the evil one, not in some neutral human determination of its own.

It is instructive to note that the Mosaic law stipulated the penalty of death for those who violated the integrity of the vow of betrothal as well as the marriage vow itself. Adultery occurs when a person who is married has sexual relation with someone other than the spouse. But it also occurs when one who is betrothed and has not yet consummated the marriage has sexual relation with someone other than the betrothed. The implication here is that an explicit contract has been made, one which is binding upon the persons involved, and in which the community itself has a stake (Deut. 22:22-27).

Yet the law did not invoke the death penalty upon those who had sexual relation and who were neither married nor betrothed. Instead, the man was bound to seek out the father of the woman and negotiate the required marriage contract with the woman (Deut. 22:28-29). In this situation the act of sexual intercourse brought no specific penalty upon the lives of those involved. However, the sexual act consummates an implicit contract that requires ratification as an explicit and public contract of marriage. One might say in this case that coitus precedes coexistence, but that coexistence contextualizes the coitus in such a way that the offense against the true order is taken up into the marriage as a responsible act of covenant partnership. This, of course, is a precarious position to be in. The distance from the "field" where the act occurred to the "father's house" where the act is contextualized constitutes a quite specific risk and danger. The couple are without support and affirmation of either family or community. Passion, and even affection, has not yet been resolved into will

91

and intention. While a "marriage" has been consummated, the coexistence that constitutes the necessary human context has not yet been made visible.

It is quite clear that the couple have come under the "command of God" through the act of sexual intercourse, questionable though it may be under the circumstances. What is required is obedience to this command through the negotiation of the appropriate wedding contract. Failure to follow through in this way then places the man and woman in jeopardy due to disobedience. The "sin" involved then is not specifically the act of sexual intercourse, though this can become the occasion for the sin, but the sin would be the failure to obey the command of God. One must not press this situation too far, but it is helpful for us to sense the distinction between responsible sexual relation and irresponsible relation. Not every act of sexual intercourse constitutes marriage — but if it does not, then it constitutes disobedience and becomes sinful. What we are arguing for here is responsibility before the command of God, not sexual permissiveness.

Theologically, marriage — not the wedding ceremony — constitutes the contextualization of sexuality as both an implicit and explicit will to coexistence. "The equation of marriage with the wedding ceremony is a dreadful and deep-rooted error," says Barth.

> Two people may be formally married and fail to live a life which can seriously be regarded as married life. And it may happen that two people are not married and yet in their precarious way live under the law of marriage. A wedding is only the regulative confirmation and legitimation of a marriage before and by society. It does not constitute marriage.[18]

The transition from affection to love to marriage and consequently to the founding of a sociological unit recognized by others constitutes the intersection of several concerns. The theological concern is for the recognition of and commitment to the form of coexistence that contextualizes the sexual life in a partnership that exists under the command of God. To this central concern there may be added the domestic aspect of marriage, which involves the severing of one domestic relation and the setting up of another. This can never take place only as a presumption of individual or even mutual interests on the part of the couple. The recognition of the new relation by parents (or by those who fulfill this responsibility) is the affirmation of the marriage by the "closest neighbors," says Barth.[19] In this sense, existing social relations (parents, children, friends) expand to create a new social unit without confusing their own relation to the marriage.

---

18. Ibid., p. 225.
19. Ibid., p. 226.

We should also consider two other aspects of marriage—legal and ecclesiastical. While the state cannot constitute marriage by declaration from a theological standpoint, coexistence in true humanity coincides with the structures of society by which order is upheld over disorder. As the manifestation of the existence of the new covenant through the life of Jesus Christ, the church affirms creation in its fundamental order. Marriage does not belong to the church as a religious institution any more than it does to the state. While Christians are motivated correctly in recognizing and desiring the affirmation of the Christian community upon their marriage, "the so-called marriage altar," warns Barth, "is a free invention of the flowery speech of modern religion."[20]

The domestic, legal, and ecclesiastical forms of recognizing marriage all enter into the "making visible" of the marriage relation as the coexistence of two people as covenant partners. We have mentioned them briefly in order to take note of their significance, but they are not our central concern. Our focus, rather, is upon marriage as that which necessarily belongs to coexistence consummated through sexual union lived out under the terms of lifelong partnership.

However, as we indicated earlier, the transition of two people into this relation is somewhat ambiguous and often precarious. What emerges here is what typically is discussed as the problem of premarital sexuality. From a pastoral perspective, it makes considerable difference whether or not one views the marital relation ethically or theologically. The person who sees marriage as the ethical validation of suspicious sexual inclinations might presume that the ideal is a totally nonsexual relationship prior to the wedding night. Those who hold this view tend to equate marriage with the wedding ceremony. However, for the one who sees marriage as the result of an encounter that involves mutual commitment to a life of covenant partnership, "premarital" will mean something other than "pre-wedding night."

At the practical level, for two persons who encounter each other in such a way that mutual love develops into a significant relationship of sharing and communion, physical sexuality may become a tyrannical and somewhat autonomous component of the relation. If the wedding ceremony itself is the only justification for having or expressing these sexual desires, there can only be a negative relation between sex and personal love. There cannot be a truly integrative motivation because, ethically, a "thou shalt not" intrudes. A dichotomy can then occur between physical expression and personal love, with unmediated guilt casting a dark shadow over the relationship. As often happens, sexual desire, disengaged from a positive integration into coexistence at the personal level, assumes an almost demonic power of its own. This, of

---

20. Ibid., p. 228.

course, proves to the one who holds an ethical view of marriage that sexual desire outside of the marriage vow is basically a negative force — not realizing that, in this case, the presupposition itself has created the fact.

From a theological and pastoral perspective, however, the goal of counseling is to enable couples prior to their wedding to sustain a basically integrative relation between physical sexuality and personal love. This includes a mutual commitment to abstinence from sexual intercourse until the time that the marriage can be consummated as a covenant partnership, upheld by God and the Christian community. In this case, abstinence is supported by the very motivations of love itself, not by setting up an ethical dichotomy.

But what is appropriate pastoral response when couples have become involved in sexual relations prior to a wedding, or have even lived together as a domestic unit prior to a formal ceremony? In this case, the integration of sexual feelings into personal expressions of love precipitates consummation of the marriage prior to its public declaration in the form of a wedding ceremony. A wise counselor will increase the contextualization of the sexual relation through enhancing the covenant partnership of the couple rather than depriving the relation of this support through ethical disapproval. How can the covenant partnership be "enhanced" in such a situation? One way is for the intentionality of the couple to become more than a mutually expressed desire to live together or to have sexual relations. In other words, the marriage has now begun in a progressive way toward its consummation in a legal and public wedding ceremony. Of course there will be tensions, and each individual situation will require unique and sensitive counsel and support. We are not suggesting here the toleration of a permissive or indiscriminate approach toward sexual relation. But neither are we suggesting that sexual intercourse itself is intrinsically immoral or evil. And it is vitally important to the health of that relation that once sexual relation has been integrated with personal love and shared life that every resource available be used to bring the relation to the optimum level of covenant partnership expressed in the conventional form of marriage. The relation is brought under the command of God at the time that it is consummated sexually, personally, and socially. This is what it means to say that "God joins them together."

WHAT GOD HAS
JOINED TOGETHER

Jesus cut through the casuistry of the legal squabbles represented by the various schools of thought concerning marriage and divorce in his own day by saying, "What therefore God has joined together, let not man put asunder" (Mark 10:9). Marriage, in the eyes of Jesus, was not a mere social contract that could be dissolved on the occasion of evidence of fraud or failure on the part of one or both parties. Rather, it comes under a divine imperative by which humans fulfill their divinely created and intended sexuality. "Marriage," says Barth, "may be defined as something which fixes and makes concrete the encounter and inter-relation of man and woman in the form of the unique, unrepeatable and incomparable encounter and relationship between a particular man and a particular woman."[21]

For Barth, this "something" that determines the encounter is the command of God. However, this command of God is not primarily a rule of marriage and only secondarily a determination of cohumanity as male and female. Rather, the command of God that determines cohumanity to be concrete existence as male or female, male and female, finds its *telos* in the particular encounter that we have defined as marriage. The sphere of the male and female is wider than that of the marriage relationship. The fundamental ethical question for the relation of male and female is thus the question of how each man and woman lives obediently in terms of the divine command. Each man and woman is finally and therefore continually under the divine determination to experience his or her own humanity through the concreteness and uniqueness of being not only a person but a male or female person. The divine command is not an arbitrary rule but a direction and promise that each person discovers and fulfills for herself or himself. Marriage is but one instance of this divine command, even though it is a most significant and consummate instance. It belongs to each person to be either male or female, but it does not belong to each person to enter into the state of marriage in order to be obedient to the divine command.[22]

Many people tend to equate the command of God with the Bible, or, more specifically, with the rules, regulations, or even principles that the Bible seems to teach. However, what we mean by "the command of God" is the demand God himself places upon us through the concrete regulations and even words in the Bible. The command of God is a summons to think, act, and live so as to be accountable to God himself, not only to conform to an abstract principle or rule. When it comes to setting forth a theology of marriage this distinction is particularly important. As Geoffrey Bromiley has pointed out, "a law of marriage differs decisively from a theology of marriage." Thus,

> we should not conclude that all that is meant by a theology of marriage exists in biblical expositions of the topic. . . . God reveals himself in and through the Bible. He speaks in and through it. Yet the Bible does not replace God. He has not just given us the Bible and left us

---

21. Ibid., p. 182.
22. Ibid., p. 140.

to it. He himself is still the one with whom we have to deal. . . . Even as we consult holy scripture, we are really consulting God himself in his self-revelation as he came and comes to us through holy scripture. God indeed says what scripture says, but this does not imply a direct equation of God and scripture.[23]

We must not misunderstand Professor Bromiley at this point. He is not suggesting that there is any other access to God than through the holy Scripture. What he is arguing is the point that God holds humans accountable to himself, not merely to a law or principle that may be abstracted from God, even though that law is supported by biblical proof texting.

In applying this argument more directly to a theology of marriage, Bromiley goes on to say that

although an account of the biblical teaching on marriage may be a theology of marriage, it will not necessarily be so. Why not? Because no theology of marriage or of anything else arises if the teaching is abstracted from God himself, if God himself is not present at the heart and center in his own relation to the topic. A theology of marriage does not consist of a mere recital of what the biblical texts have to say about it. It consists of the relating of marriage to God, or of God to marriage, as he himself instructs us through the biblical texts.[24]

This is why the command of God is the objective basis on which a theology of marriage is to be based.

The command of God is a deep and demanding summons to be human. Thus, marriage is not the command of God by virtue of its legal or moral status as determined by society. Nor is marriage equal to the command of God by virtue of a religious law upheld by the church. To live under the command of God is to recognize and assume responsibility for one's own humanity in the concrete historical situation. Because humanity is cohumanity, and because cohumanity is a divinely determined order that includes human sexuality as male and female, male or female, marriage exists within the order of cohumanity as God's purpose for the full expression of human sexuality, what the Bible calls the "one flesh" relationship. Central to this purpose is also the establishing of the responsibility to bring children into the world in such a way that they are bound to the "bonding" that exists between the father and the mother as the context of covenant love.

Clearly, the biblical teaching on marriage is that the bond of marriage actualized in the one flesh relation is not absolute. Rather, it is made relative by the eschatological truth that in heaven we shall neither marry nor be given

---

23. Bromiley, *God and Marriage* (Grand Rapids: Eerdmans, 1980), Introduction.
24. Ibid.

in marriage (Mark 12:25). The bonding between parents and children is also made relative by this same eschatological reality. Thus, Jesus warns his disciples that they must be prepared to forsake husband and wife, mother and father for the sake of the kingdom of God (Luke 14:26). When one of his followers argued that he had filial obligations at home and thus should be excused from immediately following him, Jesus rebuked him and suggested that the demands of the kingdom come first (Luke 9:57-62). We should not conclude from this that marriage is thereby not to be taken seriously inasmuch as it has only temporal and not eternal status. This would be a mistake. The command of God undergirds temporal life and calls us to responsibility in our present situation. If one undertakes marriage as a calling of God for one's life, it stands under the command of God. If one remains single as a responsible life within the context of cohumanity, this life too stands under the command of God. That is, neither marriage nor celibacy can be absolutely equated with the command of God in such a way that one or the other has a higher status.

Nor can we spiritualize the command of God in such a way that it becomes disconnected from our actual existence in cohumanity as male or female persons. Paul warns the Corinthians not to attempt to live as husband and wife without consideration for the sexual aspects of the relationships. "Do not refuse one another except perhaps by agreement for a season, that you may devote yourselves to prayer; but then come together again, lest Satan tempt you through lack of self-control" (1 Cor. 7:5). If there is marriage, then there must be consideration for the sexual relations that normally and naturally belong to the union. It must immediately be said, of course, that two people will ordinarily find their own way of expressing mutual sexual relationships within this union. The point is, one cannot deny or attempt to conceal sexuality as that which comes under the command of God as expressed in marriage. It can also be said that if there is sexual relation there must also be consideration for marriage. The command of God binds marriage to sexual union as surely as it binds sexual union to marriage. However, the apostle Paul gives pastoral counsel to the effect that there is a great deal of freedom to realize the command of God in one's own life without coming under some general "law of marriage" or "law of celibacy" (1 Cor. 7:27-38). The command of God is recognized and fulfilled within limits that are practical and possible for human persons.

Fidelity, then, as a mark of sexual integrity, is primarily fidelity to one's own sexuality as existence under the command of God. Because God has determined that cohumanity is fundamental to personal existence, and that personal existence is in each case existence as male or female, male and female, one cannot evade the responsibility to be faithful to one's own sexual identity within the framework of coexistence.[25] Marriage, too, says Barth, comes under the general category of the encounter and relationship of man and woman.[26] Therefore, the command of God is the objective basis for marriage. However, what is said of marriage in particular forms the original and primary criteria for all encounters between man and woman. In Genesis 2:24, the original determination of cohumanity is set within the context of the "one flesh" relation. While this passage may not be descriptive of the first "wedding," it is the theological and creaturely presupposition of marriage and, therefore, of the determination of all humanity as male and female.

Thus, the indissolubility of the marriage relation is due to the absolute character of the divine command, rather than to a quality or intention of human love.[27] Marriage is not subject to a universal "law" that stands by itself on the basis of an ethical "ought"; rather, the law of marriage is the result of a divine determination, understood by those who enter into the relation as a divine calling or vocation (cf. Matt. 19:11; 1 Cor. 7:17). "What therefore God has joined together, let no man put asunder," taught Jesus, as a reaffirmation of the absolute character of the divine command (Matt. 19:6). To this extent, marriage is not based on human love as its presupposition, but upon the divine command. Just what this means in the practical sense remains to be considered.

First, however, we must clarify the relation of the divine command to those who marry as well as to those who do not. Since the divine command does not relate primarily to marriage, but rather, marriage is a special instance of the divine command, we can see that marriage is a *possibility*, not a *necessity*. True, in the Old Testament marriage is presumed to be the primary duty of every person (i.e., every male). To remain unmarried was a disgrace, and to fail to have children (a son) was considered a bitter and tragic loss. The sexuality of man in the Old Testament, says Barth, "is considered almost exclusively in connexion with the procreation of the holy seed and therefore the hope of Israel.[28] Barrenness was interpreted as God's judgment upon a woman, and failure to have a son tantamount to divine rejection of a man. For this reason marriage was considered sacred. In the New Testament, however, it appears that Jesus has made marriage relative; not only by his own example of celibacy, but by his many statements that gave priority to a person's relation to the kingdom of God over marriage and family (Luke 14:16; Matt.

---

25. *CD* III/4, p. 154.
26. Ibid., p. 181.
27. Ibid., p. 185. The Reformed theologian Charles Hodge also stressed the point that a covenant is not "made exclusively by each one to the other, but by each to God. Any violation is a violation of a vow made to God" (*Systematic Theology*, vol. 3 [New York: Scribner and Company; London and Edinburgh: T. Nelson and Sons, 1891], pp. 377-78).
28. *CD* III/1, p. 312.

19:12). "The clamp which made marriage a necessity for man and woman from their creation is not removed," says Barth, "but it is certainly loosened. Marriage is no longer an absolute but a relative necessity. It is now one possibility among others."[29]

There is a valid point here for the emergence of a theology of the single person; not as a return to a call for spiritual asceticism that involved celibacy as a renunciation of sexuality altogether, but as a legitimate form of cohumanity in which one's own life as male or female is affirmed and authenticated. "The woman is the partner of the single man too," says Barth, "not woman in general, not an idea of woman, certainly not the Virgin Mary, but the concrete and definite form of woman encountering him in a particular way."[30] This partnership is not one of sexual love as in marriage, but it is no less a kinship, acquaintance, friendship, and vocation than that experienced by husband and wife. The context for this life of obedience under the divine command must surely be developed in light of the New Testament teaching concerning the entering into the present of the eschatological kingdom, where they "neither marry nor are given in marriage," and yet possess full humanity as male and female.[31] We will further elaborate on this when we consider the matter of the church as the new family of God.

LET NOT MAN
PUT ASUNDER

We must now return briefly to consider, from a pastoral perspective, what it means to say that marriage is constituted by that which "God has joined together." Barth takes the somewhat curious position that not every marriage that purports to be a marriage, either by legal action or personal action, can automatically be assumed to be a union that God has "joined together." In these cases, Barth avers, the relationship is radically dissoluble because there has been no real union in the judgment of God.[32] Certainly it does give one pause to consider extreme cases where couples are married, in a civil ceremony, foolishly, incompetently, or capriciously. Surely some of these cases must be at best only caricatures of marriage. However, can one really seriously consider the possibility that many couples in marriages that appear to be real are not, in fact, joined by God? And does this mean that in cases where marriages apparently fail and result in divorce, that this is evidence the union was not joined by God?

---

29. *CD* III/4, p. 143.
30. Ibid., p. 165.
31. Matt. 12:18-27; cf. K. Barth's commentary on this passage in *CD* III/4, pp. 296ff.
32. Ibid., pp. 208-9.

Hardly — and Barth himself will not go so far. In the last analysis, Barth says, no one can know that any particular marriage has not really been concluded by God. If one does come to suspect that there has never really been a marriage, Barth says, this can only be accepted on the ground of certain "terrible indications." And no such indication is so terrible, he adds, that it might not be fallacious.[33] So what is the point? Just this. The absoluteness of the divine commandment can never be presumed on the basis of a human will or of human love. The undertaking of a marriage relation is meant to be a serious act of recognition and affirmation of the divine command. In like manner, the dissolution of a marriage can never be undertaken on the ground of mutual intention, nor even on the failure of human love.

However, Barth goes further to suggest that in certain cases the Word of God may contain a NO that powerfully and authoritatively expresses the final condemnation of a marriage, so that one is forced to conclude that the marriage itself no longer is undergirded (if it ever was) by the divine command. In this case, dissolution by divorce is a recognition of the fact that God has already brought the marriage under the judgment of nonexistence.[34]

Thus Barth sees in the same divine commandment that makes marriage an absolute rather than a relative union God's freedom to declare in his absolute sovereignty that a marriage is a nonmarriage. This places the possibility of divorce under the condition that one can discern the will of God in a specific situation such that the scriptural statements that condemn divorce as contrary to the command of God can also be seen to support the command of God that is the basis for dissolution. Hermeneutically, this can only be understood as a theological exegesis by which universal principles are subordinated to absolute determinations of God's will. In this case, no single text can be permitted to result in a universal law of marriage that prohibits God from acting in specific, concrete situations. We can compare this approach, taken by Barth, with one espoused by Brunner, who maintains that divorce can be supported in certain cases on the basis of the law of love, which stands above the orders of creation.[35]

It seems preferable, however, to assume that all marriages recognized by state and society in general are unions in which God has joined together two people in an indissoluble relation, even in their ignorance of the divine command. This avoids the casuistry of attempting to determine which marriages have a "right" to annulment and dissolution and which do not. In this sense, no marriage can be assumed to be rightfully dissolved. However, it also confronts us with the theological reality of God's participation in and redemption

---

33. Ibid., p. 209.
34. Ibid., p. 211.
35. Brunner, *Love and Marriage*, p. 189.

of human events, including marriages. If, in fact, a marriage relationship has utterly failed to be any semblance of a covenant partnership such that the integrity of human life is not sustained but rather is being destroyed, then we have to ask the question: What does God's judgment mean on such a relation? If one determines that the judgment of God is such that the relationship no longer exists in actuality, then it might be concluded that it no longer exists in the mind of God. For to assume that the commandment of God is a reality entirely separated from concrete human existence is itself a violation of theological method. It was the nature of the incarnation that conclusively united the being of God with concrete existence. Jesus himself expressed the command of God. And what he loosed on earth was loosed in heaven, and what he bound on earth was bound in heaven (Matt. 16:19). It seems to be the responsibility of the people of God not to break the words of Jesus free from his own being, and so to make out of his teachings a universal principle, but to continue to discern the "mind of Christ" in obedience to the divine command through the reality of the Holy Spirit. Obedience to the divine command cannot circumvent the revelation of Scripture, but neither can it substitute the words of Scripture as an abstract law for the absolute command of God experienced in its terrible and yet liberating grace.

Perhaps this will help us to understand the response of Jesus to the Pharisees' demand that he speak to the issue of divorce. In allowing no place for a "rule of divorce," Jesus was not merely taking the hard line as advocated by the school of Shammai as against the more permissive and softer line of those who followed the teaching of Hillel. He was not advocating one law of divorce against another law. Nor was he even arguing for one law of marriage against another law of marriage. He rejected the concept of a "law of divorce" as not compatible with the divine command. When the Pharisees responded by asking why Moses stated that divorce was permissible in certain cases, Jesus answered, "For your hardness of heart Moses allowed you to divorce your wives, but from the beginning it was not so" (Matt. 19:8). Jesus presented the basis of marriage from the perspective of the command of God: "What therefore God has joined together, let no man put asunder" (Matt. 19:6). In saying this, Jesus removed both marriage and divorce from the status of being under a law, and reminded his listeners that humans are accountable to God himself in thought, word, and deed, not least of all in the "one flesh" relation of marriage. Viewed from this perspective, it is clear that there can be no "rules" by which marriage can be dissolved, any more than a marriage can be sanctified before God by observing certain legalities. If at times, for specific reasons, the command of God is expressed as a "law of divorce," such as Moses gave, it is immediately superceded by the command of God. Jesus, as the presence of God himself through the eternal Son, radically qualified all interpretations of the command of God by embodying it in his own person.[36]

The irony of all this is that Jesus' very words have become abstracted into a new "law of marriage and divorce." As a result, pastoral decisions on how to minister to those who suffer irreparable breakdown in their marriage are complicated by a web of casuistry involving hermeneutical hair-splitting in handling the biblical texts. Rather than hold persons accountable to God himself, and rather than be accountable to God themselves, ministers often take refuge in abstract principles that either excuse them from acting on behalf of those who are in need of support when going through the breakdown of a marriage, or free them to act in every case with little regard for the implications of their actions. In either case, they trivialize and render ineffective the commandment of God.

The command of God is always the work of God, even though it comes to expression through a regulation or rule. When the regulation or rule acts against the work of God, one is accountable to God himself, not merely to the regulation. This is what lies behind Jesus' statement "The sabbath was made for man, not man for the sabbath" (Mark 2:27). This is all the more significant when we remember that the regulation for keeping the sabbath was enforced by no less a penalty than death by stoning (Exod. 31:15). When Jesus saw that to carry out this rule without regard for God's purpose for human healing and hope was itself contrary to the work of God, he brought to bear the commandment of God in such a way that the person caught in this "legal trap" was freed and restored to life.

"The kingdom of God does not mean food and drink but righteousness and peace and joy in the Holy Spirit," taught the apostle Paul (Rom. 14:17). Yet the Old Testament clearly set forth regulations concerning the eating of food that carried the force of being the Word of God (cf. Lev. 11). But in a pastoral situation, Paul saw that the command of God was directly related to the work of God. And therefore he admonished, "Do not, for the sake of food, destroy the work of God" (Rom. 14:20). Against those who argued that they were no longer under any regulations because of their freedom in Christ, Paul taught that they were still subject to the command of God, and the command of God is to "walk in love." Against those who argued that the regulations concerning

---

36. For further references to Jesus' teaching on marriage and divorce, see T. W. Manson, *The Teaching of Jesus* (2nd ed.; Cambridge: Cambridge University Press, 1935), pp. 200ff.; Dwight H. Small, *The Right to Remarry* (Old Tappan, NJ: Revell, 1975), pp. 41ff., 142ff.; Colin Brown, ed., "Separate, Divide," in *The New International Dictionary of New Testament Theology* (Grand Rapids: Zondervan; Exeter: The Paternoster Press, 1978), 3:534-43.

food constituted the command of God, Paul taught that "he also who eats, eats in honor of the Lord, since he gives thanks to God" (Rom. 14:6).

Is it impossible for God to work in the life of one who has suffered an irretrievable loss of the "one flesh" relationship in such a way that he cannot or will not join this person together with another in a new marriage? Or, dare we suggest that the command of God can both put to death and raise again persons who experience dissolution of the marriage bond? Would it be too much to paraphrase the words of Jesus and say, "Marriage is made for man and not man for marriage?" If a theology of marriage insists that marriage is a work of God and exists under the command of God, there does seem to be a basis to suggest that in the situation where sinful humanity has experienced brokenness and loss, the commandment of God is the presence of God himself at the center of that person's life to effect new being and new possibilities. This would be to take the authority of Scripture seriously as directing us to God himself as the one who summons us in Scripture to acknowledge him as the author of life rather than of a "law that kills."

We can summarize the implications of what we have said here concerning marriage and the command of God as follows. Because God joins himself to the temporal social relationship consummated as a marriage and recognized by society and the church, that marriage is indissoluble on any grounds whatsoever other than the command of God. If a marriage comes to the point of utter breakdown so that it is a disorder rather than an order of human relationship, and inherently destructive to the persons involved, one can only seek to bring that relationship under God's judgment. For Christians, this means that the breakdown of a marriage to the point of utter failure is a betrayal of the covenant love that God has invested in that marriage, and is therefore a sin. To attempt to find legal or moral grounds on which to be excused from the marriage contract is, in our opinion, untenable. The scriptural teaching on marriage and divorce clearly brings the marriage under the judgment of God as the one who has the absolute right of determining its status.

If Christians, and the church, do not have a process to deal with sin and with grace as a work of God, then there will be little hope for those who become victims and casualties of hopeless marriages. But where the work of God is understood as his contemporary presence and power under the authority of Scripture to release those who are in bondage and create a new status where "all things are new," then the church as the community of Christ will have the courage to say NO to a continued state of disorder and YES to the forgiveness and grace of God that brings persons under a new authority of divine healing and hope. We are speaking here, by analogy, of a "death and resurrection" experience as the work of God in the midst of human lives. To create a "law of marriage" that would deny God the authority and power to put a marriage to death and to raise the persons to new life through repentance and forgiveness would appear to be a desperate and dangerous course of action. What God has joined together, indeed, let not man put asunder. But where God puts asunder as a judgment against sin and disorder, and therefore as his work, let not man uphold a law against God.

It would be misleading to end this chapter on marriage as the expression of love and sexuality on a negative note. The command of God by which marriage as a human, social relation is given the status of covenant partnership is a positive and rich resource of growth and renewal. What God "joins together" he attends with love and faithfulness. This is a promise and commitment of God himself to the marriage relation as a source of love, healing, and hope. The Christian community participates in this work of God by providing a context of support and enabling grace for each marriage that belongs to the community.

Those who undertake the calling of ministry to families through pastoral care and counseling have as their first priority the ministry of encouragement and support for marriages. This is a constructive and positive reinforcement of marriage and prevents its deterioration into a shell of the love and commitment it is meant to express. God is faithful to weak and problem-plagued marriages — not merely angry at unfaithfulness. God is patient and loving to marriages where love has been lost — not merely angry at our own anger and lovelessness. God is hopeful toward marriages that are ready to crash — not merely angry at our incompetence. God never gives up on his "joining together," because God is himself the covenant partner of marriage. This produces a bonding that never is allowed to become bondage.

CHAPTER EIGHT

UNDERSTANDING MARRIAGE: MORPHOSTASIS OR MORPHOGENESIS

I N Chapter One I suggested that modern interpretations of the family are prone to cultural bias, which often reflects both a First World or Western bias as well as a bias that protects a certain "kind" of family, usually the small nuclear family. In this chapter rather than enter into a discussion of marriage per se I would like to explore this bias from the point of view of the systemic assumptions we acknowledged in the first chapter. In order to do so we must ask ourselves two related questions: Why has this particular bias toward protecting the nuclear family developed, and is that bias necessarily biblical?

The systemic assumption that undergirds a social theology of the family recognizes the interrelationship between our assumptions about social reality and our interpretation of Scripture. In particular we are concerned with the family as a social entity, that is, as a system. Our understanding of how families work, particularly with reference to the nature of roles within the family, is determined by our assumptions about social reality — which ultimately shape how we interpret Scripture. Therefore, whenever Scripture touches upon the nature of social roles — such as the roles of husband and wife — the interpretation of that Scripture and its application to the modern world is shaped by those assumptions. All too often interpreters of Scripture derive their understanding of familial roles uncritically without determining the rules that govern social systems. What follows in this chapter is a discussion of the differing ways we can view social systems and how one's interpretation of Scripture is determined by the model of social systems one chooses. Second, I will suggest a hermeneutical principle that in my opinion allows for a more reasonable and perhaps more flexible interpretation of biblical familial roles as they might function in our changing modern world.

MODELS OF SOCIAL SYSTEMS

We begin our discussion of social reality with an overview of the various interpretations of social systems. We begin here because all interpretations of social systems are in fact representations of reality. I would suggest that most traditional approaches to the interpretation of the family are in fact a reflection of a particular sociological model or interpretation of reality; a viewpoint of a particular "school" of thought, and that other models are just as viable and should be considered as perhaps better explanations of the relevance of scriptural teaching for today.

Walter Buckley describes the three most basic models of social systems.[1] By "models" Buckley means representations of reality, the pictures that form in your head when someone says, "social systems are like. . . ."

The first model is the *mechanical model*. That is to say, social systems are said to be like machines. This view gave rise to the "social physics" of the seventeenth century, whereby man was regarded as a physical object, a kind of elaborate machine, whose actions and psychic processes could be analyzed in terms of the principles of mechanics. According to Buckley,

> in social mechanics society was seen as an "astronomical" system whose elements were human beings bound together by mutual attraction or differentiated by repulsion; groups, and their interrelations thus constituted an unbroken continuity with the rest of the mechanistically interpreted universe. All were based on the interplay of natural causes, to be studied as systems of relationships that could be measured and expressed in terms of laws of social mechanics.[2]

Representatives of this point of view would be such famous modern sociologists as George Homans and Talcott Parsons.

At the center of this concept of social systems is the principle of equilibrium. A social system is said to be in a state of balance or equilibrium when its elements are mutually interdependent in such a way that any moderate changes in the elements or their interrelations that disrupt the equilibrium are counterbalanced by changes tending to restore it. A diagram of the equilibrium model looks like this:

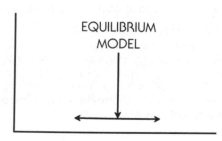

EQUILIBRIUM
MODEL

1. W. Buckley, *Sociology and Modern Systems Theory* (Englewood Cliffs, NJ: Prentice-Hall, 1967).
2. Ibid., p. 8.

According to Buckley, the equilibrium model "is applicable to types of systems which, in moving to an equilibrium point, typically lose organization, and then tend to hold that minimum level within relatively narrow conditions of disturbance."[3]

The model is essentially conservative in that whatever "is" is said to be because it "should" be. Roles, norms, and values exist as a reflection of the status quo. If, for example, we live in a social system dominated by slavery, then the roles, norms, and values of the social system seek to maintain the equilibrium by preserving slavery within the system. In other words, society should "stay the way it is" in order to preserve balance.

The major problem with the equilibrium model (or structure/functionalism as it is referred to in the social sciences) is that it does not account for change or deviance. It is fundamentally static. The social system functions so as to maintain its "patterns." It is in tension but it is stuck. As we pointed out before, what begins as "explanation" soon becomes "justification." If our model of the social system is said to be like a system of mechanics with all its parts mutually interdependent upon one another, or in a state of equilibrium, then what "is" can be said "to be" because it "should be."

Most traditional interpretations of male and female roles seem to reflect an underlying equilibrium for society. In such a model minimal change is acceptable but significant change is not. If revolution is advocated then the traditionalist will opt for the status quo. (It is interesting to note that more often than not evangelicals in the American Revolution were the Tories, and in the Civil War they fought for the South.) Radical change because it disrupts the equilibrium of the social system is considered evil, or dysfunctional, or whatever. Disequilibrium is thought of as being "of the devil."

We will look at the second model of the social system — the *organismic model* — only briefly. Here the social system is said to be like a living organism. In biological systems it is not the principle of equilibrium, as in the mechanical model, but the principle of homeostasis that is said to be what social systems are "like." Homeostasis, according to one social scientist, is

> the coordinated physiological processes which maintain most of the steady states in the organism [which are] so complex and so peculiar to living beings. . . . The word does not imply something set and immobile, a stagnation. It means a condition — a condition which may vary, but which is relatively constant.[4]

3. Ibid., p. 40.
4. W. B. Cannon, *The Wisdom of the Body* (New York: W. Norton and Co., 1939), pp. 20, 24.

Of particular importance in a homeostatic model is the organism's ability to elaborate its structure to a small degree, that is, to change so as to meet the demands of its environment. The organismic or homeostatic model can be diagrammed as follows:

ORGANISMIC
HOMEOSTATIC
MODEL

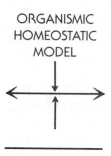

Although the organismic model is able to explain and predict change and deviance, it is not able to account for the complexity of social systems. What happens in and between social systems is infinitely more complex. The cross currents of social interaction that take place across the dinner table on a Sunday afternoon are of such complexity that the homeostatic model is inadequate. What is needed is a model that is able to account for both the parts or entities of the social system and the process or interrelationship between the parts.

The third and final model to be discussed is the *process* or *adaptive system model* of the social system. A diagram of this system looks like this:

PROCESS, OR
ADAPTIVE
SYSTEM, MODEL

According to Buckley, if the social system is like an adaptive system, then it thrives "and in fact depends on disturbances and variety in the environment."[5] Deviance and change are necessary to produce change and growth.

---

5. Buckley, *Sociology and Modern Systems Theory*, p. 40.

An excellent example of an adaptive system would be the newborn church in the early chapters of the Book of Acts. The church was in process. It was moving. There was a dynamic, a pulse beat of frenetic activity, the apostles and disciples always trying to keep up with the change. But the activity was not random; there was purpose. That is, the system possessed the capacity of being goal directed, of choosing its own ends, of elaborating its own structure under the steady hand of the Holy Spirit. What happened in the Book of Acts cannot be explained as some sort of equilibrium-seeking behavior, or an attempt to create and maintain a sense of homeostasis. Rather, what happened in the Book of Acts was the pulsing, moving of the Holy Spirit as he acted upon the social system of Palestine and brought the church into being.

In my opinion only the latter model is adequate if one is to bring the authority of Scripture to bear on the dynamic of the family, that is, to demonstrate the importance of "what was" to "what is."

THE HERMENEUTIC
OF MORPHOGENESIS

It is not possible within the confines of this chapter to fully elaborate the implications of General Systems Theory for the study of the family. Instead, we will examine the implications of two basic concepts that are discussed in the literature — morphostasis and morphogenesis. Buckley defines morphostasis as "those processes in complex system environment exchanges that tend to preserve or maintain a system's given form, organization, or state."[6] Morphogenesis, on the other hand, consists of "those processes which tend to elaborate or change a system's given form, structure, or state." Homeostatic processes in organisms and ritual in sociocultural systems are examples of morphostasis; learning, imitation, and societal development are examples of morphogenesis.[7]

It has been suggested that most interpretations of male and female roles that are traditional in nature are predicated upon an equilibrium model of social systems and are therefore conservative in nature, reinforcing the status quo. Further, in an equilibrium model biblical passages having to do with family roles are likely to be interpreted morphostatically. For example, the universal role of woman always will be interpreted to be exactly like the particulars in the biblical text. In other words, if the text is interpreted morphostatically, we will be forever looking for the exact meaning of the particulars of the text. The literal interpretation of what existed in the first century

---

6. Ibid., p. 58.
7. Ibid., p. 59.

will be taken to apply to the present. The text will be interpreted so as to preserve the system's present form, structure, or state.

There is, however, an alternative; we can apply the principle of morphogenesis. A morphogenic interpretation is one that seeks the rules that lie behind the particulars of the text. To apply a morphogenic interpretation of a text, one would seek to identify the principles underlying the text that allow for the particulars within the family roles to change in light of the present demands of the environment while preserving the principles that are applicable both then and now.

For example, consider a morphogenic interpretation of two Scripture passages: the Jerusalem Council (Acts 15) and Paul's teaching regarding masters and slaves (Eph. 6). In interpreting Acts 15, few today would teach that we should take literally the dietary restrictions James imposed. Instead, we seek the broader principle underlying the text: an appeal to unity. James's concern was to preserve the unity of the first century church as Gentile converts entered a primarily Jewish institution. In this case, then, the morphogenic interpretation allows for the continued elaboration of the social system called the church in its essential need for unity.

The second example is that of Paul's teaching regarding slaves and masters in Ephesians 6. All responsible commentators agree that slavery is an ungodly evil. However, a strict and consistent morphostatic interpretation of the text would interpret the literal particulars of the text to mean that the role of slave and master are legitimate for today, therefore preserving them. In contrast, the morphogenic interpretation applies the principle of mutual submission and mutual responsibility between employee and employer. Morphogenesis allows for the change and elaboration of the system while preserving the integrity of the system as a whole.

By way of application, then, what I am suggesting is that morphostatic interpretations of roles in Scripture are concerned with the particulars of the roles themselves. It is a fundamentally linear application. There is a direct, straight-line relationship between the roles of the first century and the family roles of the twentieth. Such interpretations tend to preserve and maintain the forms themselves even when the forms have become obsolete or dysfunctional. On the other hand, morphogenic interpretations are concerned with the rules that govern the relationships between the entities of the system. Even though the biblical particulars are no longer relevant (such as women covering their hair; see 1 Cor. 11) rules still exist for relationships between the entities of the system (such as women maintaining modesty and order in the Corinthian church).

SUMMARY AND CONCLUSION

The thrust of my argument can be summarized as follows:

1. The model one chooses to represent the realities of the social system determines the assumptions one makes about the nature of reality itself, whether that choice is made consciously or unconsciously.

2. Most traditional interpretations of family roles, especially those of husband and wife, male and female, are predicated upon the conservative functions of the equilibrium model.

3. If equilibrium is seen to be desirable, then change and deviance are seen to be evil and of the devil.

4. When it comes to the hermeneutics of family roles, we can interpret them in either of two ways: morphostatically or morphogenically.

5. If the role is interpreted morphostatically, one will pay attention to the particulars of the role itself and make an attempt to gain congruence between the essential nature of the biblical role and the essential nature of the contemporary role; this is a necessarily linear, causal process. The task becomes one of replicating, preserving, and maintaining the particulars of the system as it existed, even if the contemporary environment is unsuitable.

6. If one chooses the adaptive system model as one's representation of reality, then he will place a greater emphasis on the process of information exchange between the entities of the social or family system rather than on the nature of the entities themselves.

7. In light of the above, if one interprets the role morphogenically then what is important are the rules that govern the relationships between the roles rather than the nature of the roles themselves.

8. The roles themselves can change depending upon the demands of the environment. The authority of Scripture is never lost, however, because the rules that govern the relationships between the roles have been established and have been fully explicated.

My purpose in this chapter was to suggest the viability of modern systems theory in the process of interpreting Scripture, especially in the area of biblical teaching about family roles. The emphasis in General Systems Theory upon the importance of relationships, that is, the importance of "and," suggests the need for a similar emphasis upon relationship in the interpretation of Scripture.

In particular, I suggested the viability of the systems concept of morphogenesis over against the concept of morphostasis. It seems to me that many interpreters of Scripture in the area of family roles are selectively morphogenic when it suits their purposes and morphostatic when it does not. This is not to say that their decision is necessarily conscious; rather, it seems to take place unconsciously or at least on the level of assumptions.

One can only hope that when faced with the inconsistencies of interpretation, we will face the issues squarely and make our decisions accordingly. Our love for the Word of God and the people of God demands nothing less.

PART FIVE

FAMILY LIFE
AS A MEANS OF
SPIRITUAL FORMATION

CHAPTER NINE

SPIRITUALITY IS A DOMESTIC SKILL

A LL creatures bear a common threat to their existence by virtue of being creaturely. Creaturely life is suspended in time by the fragile mystery that binds breath to flesh and connects nerve to muscle. But no other creature experiences the double jeopardy of being human. Human existence is never assured by virtue of sustaining creaturely life. The nonhuman creatures have nothing to lose in being no more than their creaturely nature allows them to be. But humans have a destiny that, while dependent upon creaturely survival, reaches for more than creatureliness can give. Humans can live a lifetime and still fail to become what they are destined to be. In the biblical account of creation, there is a "solidarity of the sixth day" that binds the human to the nonhuman creature through a shared nature. Both are of the dust of the ground. However, the seventh day is the completion of God's creative act and the experience of God's "rest." Failure to reach this "rest" is a failure to reach the destiny God has set forth as the goal of human life and, therefore, as the fundamental orientation of life itself (cf. Heb. 4:1-13). This is what we mean when we speak of a double jeopardy in the experience of being human. Human life is not ultimately determined by nature itself, but by how one experiences the formation of the present by that toward which present life is drawn — the command and promise of God.

We have referred earlier to a theological anthropology that distinguishes between the human and nonhuman on the basis of a divine command and a divine determination. That spirit of life which determines the creaturely existence of the human is a special orientation of the unity of soul and body. The spirit of life for all other creatures is closed and self-contained. That is, their creaturely existence is identical with their spirit existence. Or, one should say, their spirit existence is contained and turned in toward their natural creaturely existence.

Human creatureliness, on the other hand, is oriented to a life and Spirit beyond the creaturely existence, and thus is not to be identified with spirit existence, though it coincides with it. It is the body/soul unity of human existence that is spiritual in its orientation and destiny. In this sense, one could say that spirit existence is identical with human existence. To be human is to exist as a body/soul unity that has a spiritual openness and orientation

115

toward the source of life itself — the Creator Spirit. To be spiritual, likewise, is to exist as a body/soul unity in which knowledge of and relation to the Creator Spirit is experienced as cohumanity. By saying this we mean to exclude all concepts of spirituality that either deny one's own humanity as a body/soul unity, or paradoxically opposes one's creaturely nature to one's human nature. The human person does not have a "higher" spiritual self and a "lower" fleshly self; no antagonism or dualism sets spirit over against flesh. When the apostle Paul introduces a distinction between fruit of the spirit and works of the flesh in his ethical admonition, he speaks of such nonphysical things as pride, jealousy, and idolatry as being works of the flesh (cf. Gal. 5:19-20). Clearly, what Paul means by "flesh" here is an introversion of spirit by which one's spirituality becomes a negative rather than a positive orientation.

Spirituality means openness of creaturely being, as opposed to closedness. Hence, spirituality is a work of love. Spirituality means human life under direction, as opposed to either randomness or senselessness. Hence, spirituality is a pilgrimage of faith. Spirituality means fruitfulness in the task of personal existence, as opposed to mere utilitarianism of being. Hence, spirituality is the realization of hope.

SPIRITUAL FORMATION
AS A HUMAN TASK

Since the nature of human existence is determined by a spiritual orientation, it follows that the development and maturation of personal life is at the same time a process of spiritual formation. The two cannot be separated. To attempt to treat the development of one's humanity by excluding the spiritual orientation of human existence is to commit the reductionist fallacy of "nothing buttery" — a person is "nothing but" the sum total of creaturely attributes and possibilities. To account for human choices as "nothing but" a stimulus response mechanism, or to explain human values as "nothing but" a conditioned psychical response either to avert pain or to seek pleasure is reductionist, a denial of humanity. Admittedly, these psychical responses and mechanisms are an important part of the creaturely function of human persons, but these components of human existence do not necessitate a closed concept of personal existence. Spirituality, as openness of being, is a necessary dimension of personal being, which is essential cohumanity — the experience of oneself in terms of the other.

For this reason, spiritual formation, as a task assigned to the process of being human, is not the imposition of an alien or parochial imperative upon otherwise complete human beings. We cannot charge the church, as a social and religious institution, with creating an extracurricular task and then seeking to bring people under its tutelage. Spiritual formation, properly understood, is intrinsic to human development. What is more, it precedes and determines whatever religious possibilities there are for human existence. Anthropologists have demonstrated that all human communities, even the most primitive, give evidence of being intrinsically religious; yet this empirical observation does not point to the intrinsic spiritual aspect of human persons. What anthropologists call "religious behavior" could very well be produced by a stimulus response mechanism at the creaturely level. I myself have seen a pet poodle taught to "say its prayers"!

Therefore, we must not mistake the imposition upon humans of an arbitrary plan or standard of behavior as spiritual formation — even if these standards of behavior are of an ideological or religious nature. "We should misunderstand the formation of man," says Bonhoeffer, "if we were to regard it as instruction in the way in which a pious and good life is to be attained."[1] Spiritual formation can no more be understood as "religious education" than it can as ideological indoctrination. Formation, rightly understood, is conformation. The original as well as the ultimate form of being human is embedded in our very creatureliness as an orientation that becomes a structure of existence. The "form" that determines human existence as both structure and goal is neither idealistic nor utilitarian. It is personal, historical, and spiritual.

Christian theology views the Incarnation of God in the man Jesus Christ as the form of the human to which all humanity must be conformed. But the Incarnation is not an ideal form that Jesus "typified" by his actions, nor a means to an end by which God could communicate his message of love and grace. Rather, the Incarnation was a creaturely and human life lived under the determination of the divine Word, fully manifesting the divine Spirit. It stands as both confirmation of authentic humanity and the goal of all personal humanity. In being conformed to the person of Jesus Christ, one's own existence as a personal and particular body/soul unity is brought to its maximum potential as a spiritual orientation of life. This is why Bonhoeffer says that

> it is not a question of applying directly to the world the teaching of Christ or what are referred to as Christian principles, so that the world might be formed in accordance with these. On the contrary, formation comes only by being drawn in into the form of Jesus Christ. It comes only as formation in His likeness, as conformation with the unique form of Him who was made man, was crucified, and rose again.[2]

The life of Christian faith carries with it an imperative for spiritual growth and discipleship, but this is a task to which every human being is summoned by virtue of existence itself. The Christian church does not add an imperative that is not already implicit in the imperative each person faces in facing life itself. To fail in this task is to lose one's own life. "For what does it profit a

---

1. Dietrich Bonhoeffer, *Ethics* (New York: Macmillan, 1965), p. 80.
2. Ibid.

man," said Jesus, "if he gains the whole world and loses or forfeits himself?" (Luke 9:25). This is the tragic imperative that shadows each person's life. One can lose one's own soul in gaining life as a natural right. This is why every person is in spiritual jeopardy, because every person is human. But there is also a positive imperative that accompanies human life: the promise and determination of God by which one can "save" one's soul. Salvation is not mere liberation from the peril of spiritual death; it is a way of life. It is the process by which one's spiritual orientation continues, in a developmental sense, to direct and to complete one's human life.

Where spiritual orientation and direction are not operative, we say, theologically, that one is a sinner and a "stranger to the covenant of promise, having no hope and without God in the world" (Eph. 2:12). In other words, one is "lost" and subject to the curse of sin, which is death. Through the activity of God's Spirit, in conjunction with the Word of God as determinative agency, however, one can experience a spiritual "rebirth" or renewal of life. This event is the beginning of a spiritual pilgrimage by which salvation is "worked out" through a human life in which the integration and realization of divine purpose takes place (Phil. 2:12). The evidences of this "spiritual growth" are called the fruit of the Spirit. Love, joy, peace, patience, kindness, goodness, faithfulness, gentleness, and self-control are characteristics of human life under proper orientation (Gal. 5:22-23). The fact that these qualities of life are confirmed only as one exists in relation to others (cohumanity) rather than as abstract and individual virtues demonstrates the fact that "spirit life" is also essentially personal and human life.

The point is this. What is termed "spiritual formation," as an imperative and discipline of Christian life and faith, is correlated with the developmental process by which individuals mature as human beings. It would seem to be more "natural" for spiritual life to have its new beginning in our personal life in connection with the process by which we also grow into persons. The dramatic exceptions to this, those in which a "new birth" is marked by a highly individualistic, psychological, and behavioral conversion experience, ought to be noted as truly exceptional rather than as normative. From the standpoint of spiritual formation itself, such experiences are actually bizarre, and if not subdued by conformation to Christ in community, can often produce "strange fruit" rather than a normative spiritual life.

This means that everything that we have said about parenting and family life is intrinsically theological. Parenting, as a function of the human family, is not true parenting unless there is openness to and interaction with the Spirit of God. Because the Spirit of God, through the humanity of God in Jesus Christ, is already intimately associated with the process of becoming human, family life as a developmental process is aligned with the task of the Christian church.

SPIRITUAL FORMATION
AS AN INTENTIONAL TASK

Because spiritual formation is closely aligned with the task of becoming human and existing in the framework of human relationships, the task of spiritual formation is lodged in the intentionality of community. This is most clearly focused in what we call family. Broadly speaking, by "family" we mean the most basic social structure within which primary and personality-effecting experiences take place with regularity and continuity. Certainly this includes the relationship of husband and wife, parents and children. But it also includes certain "extended family" situations and even fraternal and communal domestic units. To a greater or lesser degree, therefore, every person experiences a "family life" situation. Some persons, of course, have such a minimal or marginal family-life existence that they might not appear to be included in this definition. However, for the purposes of this discussion, we will assume that family life is the ordinary circumstance in which persons discover and grow into their own particular and unique spiritual being. What we will suggest here is pertinent to married couples and the nuclear family, as well as to most single adults — though, of course, with varying degrees of relevance. In a subsequent discussion we will look at the way in which the church as the "family of God" also constitutes family life and thus a means of spiritual formation.

However, we must first ask the question: Can the family really be trusted with the task of spiritual formation when it is often prejudiced by its own special interests? Will not spiritual formation then take up all the idiosyncrasies and even deformities that the family then imprints upon the helpless and malleable figure of the child?

Theodore Roszak expresses this concern poignantly when he says that

> for as long as we have been sociable animals, the burden of the family has been to stamp the young with an ancestral image and bind them to their social fate. The violation of personhood begins in the cradle, if not in the womb.[3]

It is not merely that infants are confronted with a cultural matrix that is not their choice, and that determines their own sociological orientation, but each newborn person is compromised by love itself disguised in good intentions:

> We are born into other people's intentions. We learn our names and our natures at their hands, and they cannot teach us more truth than they know or will freely tell. Can there be families whose love is not treason against our natural vocation?[4]

---

3. Theodore Roszak, *Person/Planet* (Garden City, NY: Doubleday, Anchor Press, 1979), p. 139.
4. Ibid.

Of course, one could respond by saying that there are ideals that stand above such filial parochialism, and that love is rooted in ideals, not in traditions or even in human dispositions and temperaments. But even here Roszak will not yield his point. "We know," he adds, "that every ideal that supports the family has been used to tell a lie."[5]

We must admit that love is basically intentional, and therefore spiritual formation takes place within the intentionality that lies behind acts and attitudes of love. How do we then "train up a child in the way in which he should go" (Prov. 22:6) without violating the child's basic identity and even rights as a person? Does a child have an "inalienable right" to be his or her own person without regard to the intentions of others? What is this "natural vocation" that Roszak suggests may be violated by family love?

It might be helpful to take another look at what Professor John Macmurray has told us about the intentionality that lies behind the formation of the personal. "What is characteristic of the family," writes Macmurray, "is that it is neither established by force nor maintained by a sense of duty, it is established and maintained by natural affection; by a positive motive in its members."[6] We must first consider motivations, suggests Macmurray. A community is a unity of persons who act and enact their personhood through rituals and relations that are personal as opposed to merely pragmatic or idealistic. The family is not determined by common purpose, writes Macmurray, "but only by the motives which sustain the personal relations of its members. It is constituted and maintained by a mutual affection."[7]

We may find Macmurray's distinction between motives and intentions helpful. "Though every action must have a motive," he says, "it is not determined by its motive. It is determined, as this specific action, by the operation of intention."[8] In each action of a personal agent, according to Macmurray, we must presuppose a "system of motives whose differentiations refer to the Other.... The agent can accordingly act either for or against the Other."[9] In other words, persons in relation always have motives that are differentiated in terms of the others with whom one is in relation. These motives can be either positive or negative, but in and of themselves they do not determine the relation as personal. There must be an underlying intention that is rooted in the structure of personhood itself as constituted in community. This is similar to the view I have suggested by the theological construct of cohumanity. While motives may be located in individual perceptions of the other in

---

5. Ibid., p. 149.
6. John Macmurray, *Persons in Relation* (London: Faber and Faber, 1961), p. 156.
7. Ibid., pp. 158-59.
8. Ibid., p. 110.
9. Ibid., pp. 111-12.

terms of how one views oneself, intentions are located in the structure of relation between persons. While a community of persons as constituted by intentions may be problematical due to the system of motivations that may be in operation at any given time, community itself is not problematical but is a structure of personal reality itself determinative of personal being.[10]

How does this then affect our own question with regard to the matter of spiritual formation? Can spiritual formation take place through the imposition of intentionality upon one person by another, or others, through family as community? Again, Macmurray is helpful.

> The long-range intentions which affect a child's future are taken for him; and only when he "comes of age" is he responsible, in the full sense, for his actions, and so master of his own intentions. If we consider the period of development to maturity as a whole, we must assign it a negative character, in the sense that the developing intentionality which it exhibits is itself subordinated and directed to the development of a system of motives, and so the acquirement of a system of habits.[11]

Macmurray seems to agree that a child, or even a person seeking growth into maturity, must come under a form of "tutelage" by which intentionality is learned through the rituals and habits of family or community life. This seems to include what he calls a "system of motives" that are operative for both the learner and the teacher, or the child and the parent. That is, both negative and positive motives may be present in the actions of community. The child may respond out of motives rooted in fear, or the desire to be rewarded. Parents may direct the rituals of family life out of motives rooted in insecurity or even hostility. But, if I understand Macmurray correctly, there are no "natural motives" that are intrinsic to the child such that the motives of family can fundamentally violate them. Whatever natural motives the child has from infancy on must themselves come under the tutelage of intentionality rooted in community.

This would seem to be a supporting argument for spiritual formation taking place through the rituals and structures of family life, whether in the home or through the discipling offered by the Christian community itself. This would also seem to help us distinguish between the motives operative on both sides of the spiritual formation process and the basic intentionality that determines that the formation is spiritual. That is, it is intended that the end of the process of formation leads to a competence to live in community, which is competence to love. Discipleship, as defined by Jesus, is having "love for one another," as he himself loved them (John 13:34).

---

10. Ibid., p. 162.
11. Ibid., p. 65.

Macmurray says that community is a unity of persons in which "each cares for all the others and no one for himself."[12] One cannot truthfully say that he or she loves God without also demonstrating love for the brother or sister (1 John 4:20). It is probably not true to say that competence in loving others in community necessarily leads to love of God. However, if the motives that produce love at the human level do not include the intentionality to love God as revealed through Jesus Christ, then this love is itself quite problematical. Here Roszak may be close to the truth when he says that family love may be treason against the natural vocation of the child, for, theologically, we would say that the true vocation of every person is to know and love God as Creator and Lord. Spiritual formation can be justified only when it is informed by that intentionality.

However, we have also said that the development of spirituality in the human person is linked with the development of the person as a unity of body and soul, experienced as a community of responsible love. One should not assume that "spiritual" motivations are more authentic than "nonspiritual" ones. To allow this distinction is to allow one to think that the "practice of piety" as an achievement of human community is a valid program of spiritual formation. Rather, the family which undertakes the task of spiritual formation will be transformed by the intentionality of love as an experience of God's own nature. Thus, the enhancement of family life as an intentional community through which the love of Christ is learned and practiced in day-to-day living is as good a means of spiritual formation as any other, and better than most.

SPIRITUAL FORMATION
AS A FUNCTION OF FAMILY

We turn now to the task of working out more specifically the criteria by which family life can be enhanced so as to encourage the spiritual formation of its members. If, as we have argued, one's primary experience as a social being is such that it contributes to and results in the development of true spirituality, then family life is primary to and the basis for a personal life of faith. In the same way, evidence of increased competence in family life on the part of the individual can be a sign of spiritual growth and maturity. It is not for nothing that when the apostle Paul defined spiritual maturity as a criterion for leadership in the church he included, among other things, the way in which one lived in his or her own household (1 Tim. 3:4-5).

We said earlier that spirituality means openness of creaturely being as opposed to closedness. Hence *spirituality is a work of love.* Family life con-

---

12. Ibid., p. 159.

tributes to the openness of personal being to the degree that love is an experienced reality. Jesus taught that the mark of true discipleship is love. "By this all men will know that you are my disciples, if you have love for one another" (John 13:35). The apostle John, often called the disciple of love, wrote, "Let us love one another; for love is of God, and he who loves is born of God and knows God" (1 John 4:7).

Love is more than a feeling or an inward disposition — it is an ethical task or duty. But more than that, love is ontological; its source is in the reality of personal being, which is a deeper imperative than ethical duty. Even ethicists often admit that motivations that issue from concern for the well-being of others have precedence over obedience to abstract moral principles.

There is an instructive point here. All too often we consider obedience the fundamental component in discipleship. There are, indeed, a great many Scripture texts that stress obedience as a requirement of faith and point to the obedience of Jesus to the will of the Father. However, it was the task of being a son that motivated Jesus' obedience. Thus, sonship — not obedience to ethical or ideological principles — is the ontological source of Jesus' love for the Father. When obedience is not determined by a structure of personal being, it can be demonic. There is also a discipleship of death, but it is obedience without love. Parenting must never mistake obedience itself as a positive way of producing responsibility. Obedience that does not flow from a positive relation of love, which is the source of responsible being, can only be achieved through the imposition of force and will ordinarily produce hate rather than love.

To be conformed to Christ through a process of spiritual formation, one must be open to the demand placed upon one's own life by the other. "Owe no one anything," said Paul, "except to love one another; for he who loves his neighbor has fulfilled the law" (Rom. 13:8). Here we see that the openness of being, which is a mark of the human (and therefore of the spiritual) aspect of creaturely life, is focused and committed rather than indiscriminate and promiscuous. We learn how to identify our neighbor by recognizing the one who limits our own being by his or her own presence within the circle of our existence. "I do love mankind," protested Lucy in the Peanuts comic strip, "it's people I can't stand!"

But through Jesus Christ we learn that every human being who concretely limits my life is a brother or sister, not a mere object or an anonymous instance of "mankind." To be open toward the personal being of those who occupy the same space I occupy is to be conformed to Christ. Living in such openness of being is a "work of love." This is the material content of what we mean by family life.

We can now be more specific. The relationships that place demands upon our own life through daily and domestic proximity determine to a large extent our spiritual formation, either negatively or positively. Children who live with parents experience the primary structure of spiritual formation in that relation. Husbands and wives also are necessarily linked in a relationship that involves negative or positive spiritual formation. Neither formal religious education nor spiritual exercises, either individual or corporate, can effectively replace or even overcome the lack of positive growth in these relations.

When Paul reprimanded the gross immaturity and unspirituality of the Corinthian Christians because of their atrocious behavior toward one another at the Lord's Table, he reminded them that they were to "wait for one another" when they came together to eat (1 Cor. 11). Proper practice of the basic domestic structure of their lives, he urged, would restore the spiritual integrity of their Christian fellowship. Their preoccupation with "spiritual gifts" was self-centered and unloving, in the context of their lack of family life.

This is not the place to discuss in detail the practical ways in which family life can be enhanced so as to promote recognition of those with whom we live as "neighbors." It is sufficient here to point out that this task has the highest priority in the commitment of the Christian community to spiritual formation. Our task in this chapter is to set forth the theological structure by which spiritual formation issues out of love, which is first of all domestic before it is vocational. Claims to a life of Christian discipleship are flatly contradicted where persons are not open to the personal being of those with whom one shares domestic life. Whatever practical and therapeutic help can be given to overcome such a contradiction is itself a task that enhances spiritual formation.

For the same reason, evidences of growth in competence to live openly and responsibly with others at the domestic level are signs of spiritual growth and lead directly to the kind of Christian love that Jesus said was the mark of true discipleship. Perhaps a reminder that this is true is the first step toward enhancing family life so that it actually takes place.

A second criterion of spiritual formation is that it is a *pilgrimage of faith*. When we move from love as openness of being to consider faith as life under direction, we are moving beyond the personal to the historical dimension of human life. We said at the outset of this chapter that spirituality means human life under direction, as opposed to either randomness or senselessness. This is not to imply that love is without direction, or that it is mere random movements of affection. Rather, it is the intentionality of love to encourage and develop a sense of direction in life on the part of the one loved. Love desires the freedom of the other that comes to expression as personal decision for life. Spiritual life is not only an orientation toward the other as the personal construct of reality but it is an orientation toward life itself as existence in time and space. Perhaps this is what is meant when one says that she "feels called" to do something, or has a "call" to take up a task in life. "Every man has his historical situation," says Barth.

> This is the external limitation of his vocation. In it he must always recognize the command of God and obey it.
> This historical situation is also part of the vocation of man and cannot be a matter of indifference for his divine calling and his relation to it. He is what he is here in this historical world, by it and in connexion with it.... He cannot leave it behind or shake free from it. It waits for him afresh at every stage and turning of the way. It asserts itself afresh as his special situation. It demands to be taken seriously and accepted by him. Here in his own and not another situation he must constantly find and fulfil the divine calling and command.[13]

This is certainly one of the perils that rise up to face every child who becomes open to the possibilities of life. The security and safety of being sheltered in love appear to be threatened when one opens up to the world in which one lives. From within the circle of a loving family life, the venture into the world where events are unfriendly and alien seems impossible and unthinkable. And yet, the responsibility for taking up one's own life and living it is unavoidable. But what direction should one take? How does one guess correctly when there are no apparent rules for the game? And how does one maintain trust and confidence when the rules are changed in the middle of the game?

But is this the case where there is love? Some say no, that love is not so unrealistic as to shield a child from taking responsibility, thus creating the impression that safety is found only within the "shelter" of the family. But this is so because love understands the necessity of coming under direction through faith. The point I wish to make here is that the function of a family in spiritual formation must include the orientation of each person's life upon the world as well as upon one another. Despite the fact that we experience our humanity as openness to one another, it is openness to God that is the ultimate and quintessential dimension of our being. Thus, love prepares each person to "receive his call" of God to venture into the world for his sake and for his kingdom. Here, at least, one may feel apprehension, if not dread. Parenting gives way to a "push out of the nest," so to speak. One hopes that those who have demonstrated how to love have also demonstrated what it is to live by faith. However, each person must take up the venture of faith for oneself, or else experience immobilization and lack of personal history.

Spiritual formation is linked with this stage of human development by

---

13. *CD* III/4, p. 618.

orienting one toward the concrete and historical events that make up the sequence of life itself. Where there appear to be no directions — and every crossroad is unmarked — life itself can be brought under direction and lived with faith and unswerving confidence.

Abraham stands before us as the model of a spiritual person, the father of those who have faith, because he lived a life under direction. His life was a pilgrimage of faith. All the events in his life, no matter how erratic or inconsistent, were brought under the discipline of his "calling." He was not severed from his worldly existence by the command of God, but was led into it and directed toward it. He was able to take his worldly life seriously precisely because he was under direction. Events did not determine Abraham's life in the sense of some impersonal fate; rather, he determined the meaning of events through faith in the one who called him (cf. Heb. 11:8-19).

Whereas in love there is liberation from the self to live for and from the other, in faith there is liberation from the paralyzing and immobilizing fear that arises in the face of life's uncertainties. Directedness, as a sense of divine providence in one's own life, is much more liberating than a set of directions. Directions can be misleading. The one who appears to be an infallible guide can himself become lost. Life under the freedom of the divine command, says Barth, liberates us from the ocean of everything to grasp something specific as our own. It liberates us from the tyranny of things to experience the human and personal; from demanding to receiving; from indecision to action; from anxiety to prayer.[14]

An interesting point here is how practical, specific, and directional are the "spiritual gifts" that Paul taught and the New Testament church experienced. The "charismata" are not bizarre and erratic spiritual impulses but are specific ways in which our individual lives are related to the larger body of humanity in the form of practical service. Because spiritual gifts are essentially domestic and practical, it is through family life that we must develop the competence to exercise them. Spirituality becomes technical competence as an exercise of faith. Rather than flail around indiscriminately, desperately seeking to hit upon something that will work, I put my life under direction through fitting my actions to a larger reality.

Through a healthy family life one can develop at least two things that relate directly to spiritual maturity. Both are expressed in the biblical concept of faith. One is a sense of personal destiny as determined by one's participation in a created and redeemed order, under the direction of God. The other is the discovery of the connection that links personal and historical actions to that divine order. To believe and to know that I am loved by God and called into

---

14. Ibid., pp. 664-71.

life to make that love visible through my specific actions is to live a life of faith. The domestic social unity that opens up my being to this love also connects me to the created and redeemed order. Here the rituals of family life become the liturgical forms by which worship, prayer, and service relate God to me and my life to the world in which I live. If, as we have suggested, there is a correlation between the maturity that develops through family life as a community in which the created and redeemed orders are linked to the task of personal and daily living, then spiritual formation as a pilgrimage of faith actually occurs through enhanced family life.

In the end, of course, our lives must bear the satisfaction of having been lived for a purpose that is not dependent upon our own successes or failures. We spoke of this earlier as a form of spirituality that meant fruitfulness in the task of personal existence as opposed to mere utilitarianism of being. Hence, *spirituality is the realization of hope*.

In a sense, we have already touched upon this aspect of spiritual formation. When Jesus, as the Son of the Father, discovered his own specific calling and lived it out faithfully to the end, he knew the reality of that for which he had hoped. For Jesus, hope was not some desperate gamble for a value out of which he might be cheated at the end. Rather, it was the reality of the love and calling that he experienced daily in the task he accepted as his own. For there to be fruitfulness, there must be someone to receive the fruit of our lives. For there to be hopefulness, there must be someone to ensure that the present expenditure of one's life will finally count. The realization of hope is thus a present experience, even though it is the experience of hope. How could one have deep assurance of meaning and satisfaction in life if all things were measured by what was presently possible or achieved? Abraham, we are told, died in faith, not having received what was promised (Heb. 11:13). And yet his faith was "the assurance of things hoped for, the conviction of things not seen" (Heb. 11:1). In the face of the continual threat of loss each person experiences in some way, the only meaning would seem to be a desperate denial of meaning — but this is the way toward nihilism, as existentialist philosophy has taught us.

At the end, the apostle Paul could say, "I have fought the good fight, I have finished the race, I have kept the faith. Henceforth there is laid up for me the crown of righteousness, which the Lord, the righteous judge, will award to me on that Day" (2 Tim. 4:7-8). Paul experienced a deep sense of satisfaction with the life he had lived. His hope was not for compensation for an unsatisfactory life; rather, it was the realization of that very life which he had lived under divine direction. Despite the tears, the trials, and even the mistakes, Paul testifies that his life was finished, that it did not need to be completed by something that did not really belong to him. He has the assurance that his life counted for something, because it counted for his Lord. The personal knowledge and satisfaction that one's life is the realization of everything that one could have hoped for is surely a mark of spiritual formation. But how is it possible to say that? Do not each of us feel deprived of opportunities and experiences that we crave and seek as a greater fulfillment? Have not each of us also lost some things — irretrievably, by our own estimation — for which there is no compensation?

Yes, it would seem so. But then what does it mean when Jesus says, "He who loses his life shall gain it"? And what does it mean when Paul says, "but whatever gain I had, I counted as loss for the sake of Christ.... Let those of us who are mature be thus minded" (Phil. 3:7, 15)? Who will teach us the difference between the gain that cannot be lost and those losses that rob us of nothing that is finally and ultimately significant?

Who will teach the child born with a twisted body that life is a gift to be accepted and valued? Who will bring a child who once saw clearly to see the goodness of a life to which he is now blinded? Do you doubt that it can be done? Then you have not known the same people that I have known. Is bitterness and defiance more human in the face of deprivation than forgiveness and acceptance? Is harbored resentment at life's unfairness and manifest dissatisfaction with one's own life more spiritually mature than a cooperative and loving spirit? No? Then why is the Christian religion so powerless to transform such lives through proclamation and teaching? Because unrealized hope cannot be healed by words that do not touch the pain and emptiness we all feel to some degree.

Good parenting and a participation in family life that itself is a liturgical reenactment of the created and redeemed order must do this. And it can, because it has the power to awaken in us the mystery of being human in such a way that we can grasp the reality of our own humanity as the object of God's love and care. Somewhere, sometime, some way, each person must have a line drawn around his or her own existence that says, "This life of yours is sufficient to last through all eternity, though you will experience many insufficiencies; this life of yours is complete, though not all parts of you are completely finished." But this can be said only when one is sure that God does indeed love as he says he does, that God does truly complete each act of his love, and that the Word of God that we have already heard and believed is the final Word, and thus the ground of our hope.

> The Lord is my chosen portion and my cup;
> Thou holdest my lot.
> The lines have fallen for me in pleasant places;
> yea, I have a goodly heritage.
>
> (Psalm 16:5-6)

CHAPTER TEN

CONTENT AND CONTEXT
IN THE SPIRITUAL FORMATION
OF CHILDREN

O FTEN in the twenty-plus years I have been studying Scripture and what it says about family matters, I have questioned the meaning of Scripture as it deals with particular issues of interest to secular family literature. One such period of questioning and puzzlement concerns the interpretation of Paul's letter to the Ephesians, where he discusses the roles of parents and children. What I would like to suggest in this chapter is that in his instructions to parents Paul gives us an outline delineating what is at the heart of the parental task of the spiritual formation of their children. My suggestion is supported by a significant secular research project measuring parent/adolescent interaction, which I will discuss in the remainder of the chapter.[1]

EPHESIANS 6: 1-4
A MODEL FOR THE
SPIRITUAL FORMATION OF CHILDREN

A discussion of Ephesians 6:1-4 begins not with verse one and the responsibility of the child but with verse four and the *responsibility of the parent*, in particular the responsibility of the father. According to Paul, parents bear two major responsibilities: to raise their children in the discipline of the Lord and to raise them in the instruction of the Lord. The two key words are *discipline* and *instruction*, both of which are under the qualification of being "of the Lord."

The word we translate as *discipline* in the New Testament is the Greek word *paideia*, which means to control the direction of or to harness the energy of, as one controls a horse through the use of a bit. It also means to control in the sense of controlling the direction of a plant through the judicious

---

1. I first reported my reflections on this research in the popular magazine *Family Life Today* 1 (Jan. 1975) in an article entitled "What Kind of Parent are You?"

use of pruning.[2] Whether it refers to the hand of the boatman on the tiller of the ship, the rider manipulating the bit in the horse's mouth, or the gardener pruning the young vine so as to produce new and productive growth, *paideia* means to "control."

If we were to think of control as describing a relationship distributed along a continuum, then at one extreme would be permissiveness and at the other punitiveness. What the apostle is trying to instruct the Ephesian church about parental control probably would fall somewhere toward the center of the continuum.

The second major responsibility of the parent is to raise the child up in the "instruction of the Lord." The word we translate as *instruction* is the Greek word *nouthesia*. It is a compound word derived from two other words, *nous* or mind, and *titheme*, the word meaning "put" or "place." Thus, the import of the word is to put or to place something in the mind.[3]

Nouthesia has another, more subtle dimension that we need to mention here. This has to do with its quality of gentleness. We can illustrate this by describing the work of a rice farmer. Anyone who has ever seen rice farmers plant their crop are especially aware of the toil and tenderness associated with the process. One by one each individual shoot is placed in the ground under the water and tapped in with the hand and feet of the planter. It is back-breaking, painstaking work. When the field is planted and the farmer stands back and surveys his or her work, it is a spectacular sight. In what was once a smooth pond or small placid lake the planted rice protrudes through the surface of the water evenly in rows, with just enough of the plant showing to allow it to catch the warmth of the sun. Words like "careful," "tender," "orderly," and "gentle" leap to the mind when describing the process. So it is with the "instruction of the Lord." The word "instruction" has a caring, loving, and gentle quality to it.

Again, if we were to think of this as a process along a continuum, at the one end would be something like neglect and at the other would be a smothering kind of overattention. Whatever "instruction" means, it probably means something between neglect and smothering attention.

Finally, we should look briefly at the meaning of the phrase "of the Lord." We can interpret this as either a body of truth that comes from the Lord (if the Greek phrase is seen as a subjective genitive) or that which leads the child to the Lord (if the phrase is an objective genitive). The first meaning emphasizes a specific lesson that God intends parents to communicate to their chil-

---

2. See G. Bertram, "paideia," in the *Theological Dictionary of the New Testament*, ed. Gerhard Kittel and Gerhard Friedrich (Grand Rapids: Eerdmans, 1967), 5:596-625.
3. See J. Behm, "nouthesia," *TDNT* 4:1019.

dren, while the second emphasizes a direction in which the Lord would have the child move, based upon the way in which the child is disciplined and instructed.[4] That is, the first places the emphasis upon a specific content in the sense of information, and the second places an emphasis upon a unique context, one designed to motivate the child in a particular direction.

For the purposes of the present chapter, we will focus on the latter definition as the better interpretation, especially when confronting the issue of spiritual formation of children and adolescents. As we will see later, the context of parenting is fundamentally and ultimately more important than content, not only when it comes to the communication of religious beliefs and practices but also when it comes to most of what touches the life of a child.

What, then, are the *responsibilities of children* to their parents? Paul's injunction to children is that they "obey" their parents. The word we translate as *obey* is the Greek word *hupakuo*. Its etymology is rooted in the word *akuo*, to "hear" or to "listen." The same root word underlies the English word *acoustic*, having to do with sound. The implication of the Greek word is that the essence of obedience is to hear and to listen and then to respond appropriately.

Parenthetically, in terms of the issues of the parental tasks mentioned above, the question we must ask ourselves in terms of spiritual formation is what kind of parent is more likely to have children who listen and respond, especially to the things of the Lord?

What intrigues me in this passage of Ephesians is Paul's use of two Old Testament quotations, the first from Exodus 20:12, " 'Honor your father and mother' (this is the first commandment with a promise)," and Deuteronomy 5:16, " 'that it may be well with you and that you may live long on the earth.' " This raises the question, Why does Paul use these two passages and the truths they seem to set forth and not say something else? In other words, what is the relationship between a child's obedience to parents and his or her sense of well-being and living long on the earth?

In pursuit of an answer to my question I explored every commentary I could find in a graduate seminary library. Much to my surprise, as I took volume after volume off the shelf and found the passage in question, author after author either simply did not deal with the issue or did so in a way that left me with the question still unanswered. Unfortunately, such is often the case in matters dealing with the family from a biblical as well as social and behavioral sciences perspective.

I have learned at those times to put such questions on the back burner

---

4. See. H. E. Dana and J. R. Mantey, *A Manual Grammar of the Greek New Testament* (New York: Macmillan, 1927), pp. 73-81.

of my unconscious and to ask the Holy Spirit to bring the answer to my consciousness by whatever means and in such a way that I know and can recognize the answer. Thus, I have become increasingly aware that answers to questions about what Scripture is really saying about the family are to be found not only in traditional sources, such as commentaries on Scripture and treatises about theology, but also in empirical research from the social and behavioral sciences. It is true, then, as Baum suggested, that theology should look for paradigms in disciplines other than philosophy. In this case my training as a family sociologist and the paradigms used in that discipline proved to be most helpful.

FAMILY SOCIALIZATION:
A PARADIGM FOR PARENT/CHILD INTERACTION

All of this came into focus for me at a National Council of Family Relations annual conference. A paper read at a workshop on Theory Construction presented the research findings of a major project undertaken at the University of Minnesota.[5] As the project was reported by three of the four researchers, I became aware that what they had discovered in their empirical quest bore directly upon my questions regarding Paul's teaching in the Book of Ephesians and the parent/child relationship. What follows is a description of that study.

We can define *socialization* as "the process by which persons acquire the knowledge, skills, and dispositions that make them more or less able members of their society."[6] The researchers at the University of Minnesota sought to identify those ways in which the family in general and parents in particular act as agents of socialization for their young. They chose to study adolescents as their research population and to measure the effects between the quality of their relationship with their parents and four areas pertinent to their adolescent well-being.

The research subjects were more than 2,600 high school young people from four metropolitan centers in the United States, with two samples from Puerto Rico and Mexico. The project constitutes one of the largest cross-cultural studies concerning family socialization ever undertaken.

The two parental dimensions chosen as the independent variables in the study were the dimensions of support and control, which were mentioned in

---

5. A. J. Weigert, D. L. Thomas, and V. Gecos, "Family and Socialization: A Quest for Theory," an unpublished paper presented at the Annual Meetings of the National Council of Family Relations, October 1972.

6. Orville G. Brim and Stanton Wheeler, *Socialization After Childhood* (New York: John Wiley and Sons, 1966).

earlier literature by Murray Straus.[7] These two terms, *control* and *support*, as defined in the study, have meanings similar to words we have discussed. *Control* is "that quality of interaction which is perceived by the child as constraining him to do what the socializing agent wants." Note the similarity between the Greek word *paideia* and the research definition of control. *Support* is "that quality of interaction which is perceived by the child as establishing a positive affective relationship between him and the socializing agent."[8] Again, we can see a similarity between this definition and our definition of *instruction* mentioned above.

Operationally, the dimensions were responses of the adolescents to two Likert measurements taken from the Cornel Parent Behavior Description Inventory. The control response was: If I don't do what is expected of me, s/he is very strict about it; s/he keeps pushing me to do my best in whatever I do; s/he expects me to keep my things in good order; s/he keeps after me to do well in school. The support response was: If I have any kind of a problem, I can count on him or her to help me out; s/he says nice things about me; s/he teaches me things I want to learn; s/he makes me feel s/he is there if I need him or her.

The four dependent variables were measurements of the adolescents themselves. They were: general self-esteem (i.e., what is their sense of self-worth); conformity to authority figures in the community (i.e., how well do they think they get along with authority figures other than their parents, such as teachers, the police, etc.); religiosity (i.e., how well or poorly do they embrace the religious beliefs of their parents); and conformity to the counterculture (i.e., do they see themselves as belonging to or not belonging to whatever is the dominant youth counterculture in their community).

The research strategy of the study sought to measure not only the direct effects of parental control and support upon the teenagers but also to measure the effects of interaction between them. The figure listed below represents the rotation of the independent variables into a circumplex along with the terms used to describe the four quadrants created by the rotation. The four descriptive categories are taken from Baumrind's work with young children and their families.[9] The effect of the independent variables of parental control and support upon the four dependent variables are reported in the parentheses in their rank order, with (1) representing the highest or best score and (4) the lowest or poorest score. We should note that the counterculture scores are just the

7. M. A. Straus, "Power and Support Structure of the Family in Relation to Socialization," *Journal of Marriage and Family* 26 (August):318-26.

8. Weigert et al., "Family and Socialization," p. 5.

9. Diana Baumrind, "Current Patterns of Parental Authority," in Developmental Psychology Monograph Series, vol. 4, no. 1, pt. 2.

opposite, with (1) equaling highest identification with the counterculture and (4) equaling the lowest.

According to the researchers, "by far the strongest and most consistent finding is the power of the support variable. The effect of support from each and both parents emerges as the major contribution of this research across a variety of samples and dependent variables."[10] In the case for each dependent variable the better scores were associated with higher support.

The Minnesota Study substantiated my suggestion that context is more important than content in the spiritual formation of children, as the researchers found that

> a similarly strong pattern emerged in the positive relationship between support from either parent and the adolescent's religiosity. There are qualifications, however. Support is unrelated to religious knowledge in all of the samples and to all dimensions of religiosity in the Mexican sample. The relationship is strongest for religious practice and belief, and for the Anglo samples. There seems to be no clear dominance of the impact of support from one parent rather than the other.[11]

Looking at the control variable, it is interesting to note that whether the parent demonstrates low or high control, the numbers are fairly consistent. However, given the focus of the present chapter, we should note that the Authoritarian quadrant has the lowest scores for conformity to authoritative others and religiosity, especially under father conditions.

Here we should remember Paul's warning in the first part of Ephesians 6:4, "Fathers, do not provoke your children to anger." Certainly there is a high price to be paid by the adolescent if the parent is highly controlling while at the same time demonstrating low support. In each of the dependent variables, it would be better for the adolescent in terms of the findings of this study for an emphasis to be placed upon support rather than control. I am reminded of the encouragement in the Book of Hebrews that "the Lord disciplines him whom he loves" (12:5-6). Perhaps one way to think of God as Father is to think of him as an authoritative parent who has the ability to relate to us supportively without losing control.

In terms of the original question that provoked me to action, that is, what is the relationship between a child's obeying its parents and a sense of well-being, the research is pregnant with implications. Two points in particular are worth mentioning. First, I'm sure that the apostle Paul anticipated at least logically that the kind of parent a child would be expected to obey would be

---

10. Weigert et al., "Family and Socialization," p. 8.
11. Ibid., p. 10.

Figure 1:
*Summary of Findings on the Joint Effects of Control and Support on
Adolescent Characteristics*

HIGH SUPPORT

Permissive Parents

A. General Self-esteem (2)
B. Conformity to Authoritative
   Others (2)
C. Religiosity (2 for Anglo samples with
   some mixture, and 1 for San Juan)
D. Countercultural Identification (some
   mixing of 2 and 3, with a tendency
   to 3 for females)
In general, medium/high on dependent
variables

Authoritative (Democratic) Parents

A. General Self-esteem (1, especially self-
   worth)
B. Conformity to Authoritative Others
   (1, especially for parents)
C. Religiosity (1)
D. Countercultural Identification
   (tendency to 4)
In general, highest on dependent
variables, and most consistent in ranking

LOW CONTROL ——————— HIGH CONTROL

Neglectful Parents

A. General Self-esteem (4)
B. Conformity to Authoritative Others
   (mixture of 3 and 4, with tendency
   toward 4 for parental condition)
C. Religiosity (mixture of 3 and 4 with a
   tendency toward 4)
D. Countercultural Identification
   (tendency toward 1 for females and 2
   for males)
In general, lowest on dependent
variables, except for males under father
condition

Authoritarian Parents

A. General Self-esteem (3)
B. Conformity to Authoritative Others
   (mixture of 3 and 4, with clear
   pattern for Anglo males under father
   condition and Latin males under
   mother condition to rank 2)
C. Religiosity (mixture of 3 and 4, with
   tendency for Anglo males under
   father condition to rank 4)
D. Countercultural Identification
   (mixture of 1 and 2 for females with
   clear pattern for males to rank 1)
In general, medium/low on dependent
variables except for males under father
condition

LOW SUPPORT

135

the healthily supportive and controlling parent described in Ephesians 6:4. Second, if the conclusions of the University of Minnesota research mean anything, the study is in essence saying that children of supportive parents who care about them and who have the ability to communicate that care so that the child feels loved are likely to experience a better sense of self-worth, to associate better with others in the community, and to be less likely to get involved with the destructive life-styles of the counterculture. There is every reason to believe that "it will be well with them," and that they will "live long in the land."

CONCLUSION

I have come to the conclusion that spiritual formation in the confines of the family is at its heart a socialization task. This means that whatever affects the ability of the family to fulfill its function as the primary socialization agent in the life of its children ultimately affects the ability of the parents in particular to lead their children meaningfully along the road or journey of faith.

In particular, the research developed at the University of Minnesota serves to remind us of the scriptural teaching that parents in general and fathers in particular are keys in the spiritual formation of their children.

In my opinion, it is the task of the church to act both prophetically and supportively of parents toward this end. Prophetically, we are to challenge parents to be integrally involved with the task of the spiritual formation of their children; supportively, we are to provide whatever instruction they need to do their job and do it well. Perhaps the task of the church is to parent the parents. To this end, I suggest an emendation and amplification of Ephesians 6:4:

> Leaders of the church, do not provoke parents in such a way that they provoke their children to wrath. Instead, direct their behaviors so that they might direct their children appropriately. You must also become instructors of instructors — of parents who will, we hope, teach their children to love God.

PART SIX

THE CHURCH AS THE NEW FAMILY OF GOD

CHAPTER ELEVEN

BROTHERS AND SISTERS, WE SHALL ALL BE THERE!

W AS Jesus disloyal to the hallowed institution of the family? Or, to put it another way, did Jesus undermine the family—first, by his own example in choosing the celibate life and, second, by teaching a radical discipleship that set a person at odds with father or mother, brother or sister, for the sake of the kingdom of God? "For henceforth," said Jesus, "in one house there will be five divided, three against two and two against three; they will be divided, father against son and son against father, mother against daughter and daughter against mother" (Luke 12:52-53).

Perhaps the question should be put in still another form. In light of Jesus' teaching concerning the new order that exists in the kingdom of God, can the Christian church today make family life a means of spiritual formation, and the building of the family its central task? Is there, in fact, a basic contradiction in exalting the natural family as a paradigm of spiritual development while at the same time urging Christians to take seriously the claims of Christ and enter into a life of discipleship that demands undivided loyalty to his cause and his community?

This is not an idle question, put forth to tease the mind and provoke the spirit. We have asserted unequivocally that a person's spiritual life is evidenced most clearly by openness and commitment to others with whom he or she shares domestic space. Does this book on a theology of the family now come to grief over the teachings of Jesus himself? In the final analysis, are our commitments to family life and to Christian discipleship irreconcilable?

It will do little good to pass over the questions raised by Jesus' teachings and look for comfort from the apostle Paul! While he advocated marriage for those unable to contain their sexual desires, he also believed that Christians were better off single, as he was, not frustrated and hindered in their discipleship by domestic trials and tribulations that come with marriage and will all too soon pass away when the Day of the Lord comes (1 Cor. 7:8-40).

Therefore, is Christian discipleship—as apparently taught and modeled by both Jesus and Paul—compatible with our emphasis on family life? I believe it is, despite what seems to be a very real contradiction. Thus, we must look more closely at the teachings of Jesus in this regard.

139

JESUS' TEACHINGS ON FAMILY
AND THE KINGDOM OF GOD

What is Jesus proclaiming in his pronouncements concerning the radical claims that the kingdom of God makes on every natural order, including the institutions of marriage and family? Certainly it is not a proclamation that dissolves the basic social relation between people. On the contrary, Jesus teaches that the commandment to love your neighbor as yourself is of equal importance with the other supreme commandment to "love the Lord your God with all your heart, and with all your soul, and with all your mind, and with all your strength" (Mark 12:28-31). He does not dissolve the natural order of family, though he qualifies it as an absolute and brings it into the service of the new order, which is itself the original order.

This does not question the relationships between husband and wife, parents and children, brothers and sisters as such. What is questioned in these sayings, says Barth, "is the impulsive intensity with which he [the disciple] allows himself to be enfolded by, and thinks that he himself should enfold, those who stand to him in these relationships."[1] Rather, it is one's captivity to these relationships that is questioned. Family structures can be a clannish imprisonment of the person no less than material possessions or worldly fame. Jesus' proclamation is a message of liberation from these relationships as an absolute demand over the Christian disciple. Thus the excuse of the invited guest, "I have married a wife, and therefore I cannot come," is to be seen precisely on the same level as those whose purchases of land or oxen claimed their prior interest (Luke 14:18-20). In a similar situation, Jesus gives a remarkable answer to the man who was considering discipleship: "Leave the dead to bury their own dead; but as for you, go and proclaim the kingdom of God" (Luke 9:59-60).

To this series of teachings belong the other provocative sayings about "leaving," "dividing," "disuniting," and even "hating." Jesus has come not to reaffirm the status quo and so to "bring peace." If a person loves father or mother, son or daughter more than him, Jesus says that that person is not worthy of the kingdom of God (Matt. 10:34-38). When Jesus requires one to "hate" his father and mother, even his own life, he warns against setting out to build a tower or go to war without taking stock of what the cost will be. Those who are preoccupied with entanglements that will eventually cause them to abandon the kingdom of God have not really been liberated by the kingdom of God.

Love of neighbor is the other side of the coin from love of God; it is not

---

1. *CD* IV/2, p. 550.

a coin with its own realm. The coming of the kingdom of God means the end of the absolute hold that the natural order has over the person who is first of all the object of God's love and determination. In a sense, one could say that the Sabbath is a renunciation of all other principles that hold good for the first six days. The Sabbath is a liberation from all natural powers that seek to determine one's destiny, in order that one's destiny may come under divine and supernatural determination.

Jesus proclaims the disciple's freedom from general law and universal principles in order to fulfill life in concrete obedience to the law and Word of God. We must remember that in the Old Testament, marriage and family are portrayed generally in terms that seem to bring divine reproach upon the unmarried or barren woman and divine disfavor upon the man who does not father a son. The very fact that Jesus himself does not marry and have a son is a remarkable challenge to this established tradition and general "law." Yet he claims the gift of God upon his life and experiences liberation from the general law in order to fulfill faithfully his specific calling.

This is how one should also view Paul's somewhat ambivalent view toward marriage and family in his first letter to the Corinthian church (1 Cor. 7). While it is true that marriage is a "gift of God," Paul teaches further that each person — married, single, separated, or widowed — has his or her own particular gift (*charisma*) from God (1 Cor. 7:7). The old order is not allowed to invoke its taboos against either singleness or barrenness. One is really free to marry, not out of fear that one will not inherit some blessing from God or will lose one's own claim on posterity, but in faith and love. But one is also free not to marry and yet experience God's blessing.

In a certain sense, contemporary Protestantism also may have capitulated to an implicit "general law" concerning marriage and family life as having special divine favor. "Protestantism," says Barth,

> in its fear of the bogy of monasticism . . . has very radically ignored this proclamation of Jesus Christ, as also that of other freedoms. To a very large extent it has acted as though Jesus had done the very opposite and proclaimed this attachment — the absolute of family. Can we really imagine a single one of the prophets or apostles in the role of the happy father, or grandfather, or even uncle, as it has found self-evident sanctification in the famous Evangelical parsonage or manse?"[2]

Well, hardly! Though it is not outside the realm of possibility that even the apostle Paul occasionally visited Tarsus with salt water taffy purchased in Corinth for his nephews and nieces, whose own lives were deeply touched by their "Uncle Paulus." We simply do not have the entire picture of what domestic

---

2. Ibid., p. 551.

life was like for the apostles, even though we certainly can assume that it was marginal compared to most.

The point is this. Even as the human exists in an indirect relation to the natural order by virtue of a direct relation to the Word of God as source and sustenance of life, so the Christian is related indirectly to natural relationships and directly to Christ. God was never an indirect and consequential partner with Adam and Eve. Rather, he was the direct source of their own consequential relation to each other. It was for this reason that we discussed parenting as logically and theologically prior to family. And for the same reason, we did not discuss family under a general category, but as that which indirectly represents the parenting of God as Creator and Lord.

When Jesus calls us to discipleship, says Bonhoeffer,

> we learn that in the most intimate relationships of life, in our kinship with father and mother, brothers and sisters, in married love, and in our duty to the community, direct relationships are impossible. Since the coming of Christ, his followers have no more immediate realities of their own, not in their family relationships nor in the ties with their nation nor in the relationships formed in the process of living. Between father and son, husband and wife, the individual and the nation, stands Christ the Mediator, whether they are able to recognize him or not. We cannot establish direct contact outside ourselves except through him, through his word, and through our following of him. To think otherwise is to deceive ourselves.[3]

However, Bonhoeffer adds,

> The same Mediator who makes us individuals is also the founder of a new fellowship. He stands in the centre between my neighbor and myself. He divides, but he also unites. Thus although the direct way to our neighbor is barred, we now find the new and only real way to him — the way which passes through the Mediator.[4]

Now we can conclude that, rather than there being a contradiction between the family and the kingdom of God, there is a correlation and even a symbiotic relationship. The demands of the kingdom preempt the demands of filial and family relationships indirectly, not directly. The same God who has established family as the basic unit of human social existence is the Lord to whom each family and each family member owes worship and obedience. Jesus came preaching a gospel of the kingdom of God (Matt. 4:23). There is also a gospel of the family, which Jesus proclaimed through his own participation in and upholding of the filial and domestic relationships in his own

---

3. Dietrich Bonhoeffer, *The Cost of Discipleship* (London: SCM Press, 1959), p. 86.

4. Ibid., p. 90.

life. One of the last words from the cross takes account of this filial relationship, wherein Jesus made provision for his mother by designating the beloved apostle, John, as her son, and her as his mother (John 19:26-27). There is a gospel of the family as well as a gospel of the kingdom.

What we see in the teaching of Jesus is not an essential contradiction between family and kingdom but rather a tension that takes two forms, positive and creative or negative and destructive. The first point of tension between family and kingdom, which is positive and creative — even re-creative — is grounded in the original tension between the sixth day of creation and the Sabbath as God's day of rest. The six days of God's creating are reflected in the command that "six days you shall labor . . . but the seventh day is a sabbath to the Lord your God" (Exod. 20:9-10). The structure of family life is linked closely with the sixth day, but the quintessence of family life is linked with the seventh, which represents the paradigm of covenant as the quintessence of family (see Chap. 3). Thus, a creative and positive tension exists between family as a social reality of the sixth day and family as a covenant reality of the seventh day. The family is not an "order of creation" in the older sense of having its own natural order and laws that give it independent status over and against the kingdom of God. To the degree that family is also a part of the "created orders," it has its own place and purpose within this created structure. But the created order does not yield any law of the family that is not superceded by the Lord of the family.

We see this tension reflected at certain points in the New Testament. For example, when the apostle Paul suggests that it might be preferable not to marry and so to assume the responsibilities and duties that accompany such a relation, he has in view the impending dissolution of all created orders by the new order inaugurated by the resurrection of Christ and hastening to its consummation at his return. In Paul's mind, the "appointed time has grown very short" and consequently one should live with a view to serving the Lord with undivided attention (1 Cor. 7:29-31). This frees marriage and family from bondage to a natural or biological determinism, while at the same time places it within a new context of covenant love and responsibility.

The second level of tension is between order and disorder, and this cuts right through both covenant and creation as humans experience them. The effects of the fall of Adam and the consequent disorder that infects every personal form of existence from Adam to Christ (but does not include him) brings defeat, frustration, destructiveness, and bondage into human relationships. It is this latter distinction between order and disorder that is absolute and lies behind the polemics of both Jesus and Paul against "nature" and even natural institutions. For under the tyranny of sin and disobedience, the natural becomes unnatural and even demonic. The liberation of creation from disorder so that the covenant order may be reestablished is often convulsive and uncompromising.

Failure to distinguish these two levels of tension leads to the confusion between renunciation and redemption. The creation order is redeemed, not renounced. The Sabbath is for man. That is, God seeks the true creaturely order as he determined it to be. So then, marriage and family life are first of all qualified by the relation between covenant and creation, and second are brought under the redemptive and mediating work of Christ. Because Jesus represents the presence of the kingdom of God as the eschaton, or the end of the old order, there is an eschatological tension as well in his proclamation. In light of the new order that is inaugurated by the kingdom of God as present in Christ, a radical judgment is pronounced upon existing orders that seek to bind humanity to the old.

Was Jesus disloyal to the institution of marriage and family? Of course not. He continues to be the Lord of the family, who desires that each family experience and embody the righteousness, joy, and peace that belong to those who have received the kingdom of God. What remains for us is to trace out the way in which the church, as the new family of God, enhances and upholds family life by exorcizing the destructive and demonic disorder that threatens it, and by re-creating it into the new order of God's covenant community.

THE CHURCH AS FAMILY

The message of the good news, which became the hallmark of the New Testament church from its very inception, is the announcement of the new covenant community being formed in Christ. The corporate life of the church, immediately following Pentecost, experienced a communal life with a domestic character. In describing those first believers, Luke recalls that "day by day, attending the temple together and breaking bread in their homes, they partook of food with glad and generous hearts" (Acts 2:46). This commitment to each other as brothers and sisters in a new community of love and faith captures exactly the import of Jesus' own teaching.

> "Who are my mother and my brothers?" And looking around on those who sat about him, he said, "Here are my mother and my brothers! Whoever does the will of God is my brother, and sister, and mother." (Mark 3:33-35)

New filial relations are created between those who were once strangers and unrelated. Paul properly calls Christ the "head" of this new community, his Body (Eph. 1:22-23). And yet, Christ is himself the Body in which individual members now have their identity as his brother or sister. From a theological perspective, the individual's new personal identity as one who has experienced the salvation of God is formed through a common existence in Christ's Body. This commonality, or *koinonia*, binds each person to Christ and one to another. As a consequence, failure to love the brother or sister is to break fellowship with Christ himself (1 John 4:20).

Parenthetically, we should note here that this new family of God, constituted as the *koinonia* of Christ, is itself the original order of humanity as portrayed in the covenant people of Israel. The primal reality recognized in the Old Testament is the community — the corporate, social reality. In Israel, "individual and community are held together in a viable relationship without either being lost in concentration upon the other. Yet the formation of the community is God's central act."[5] Seen against the backdrop of the ancient tribal view of human social existence, the Old Testament concept of the individual-in-community as determined by the covenant of Yahweh clearly breaks with the natural order. The life of Israel proclaims to the nations a transcendent basis for human existence and qualifies the natural, clannish, or tribal view.[6] For this reason, proclaims the creation account, "a man leaves his father and his mother and cleaves to his wife" (Gen. 2:24).

The filial bond, formed as a biological or natural order, gives way to the higher demand of covenant partnership. Or, one could say, consanguinity as the basis for family gives way to consensuality.[7] Consanguine relationships rest upon blood ties, and one's participation in the relationship is not premised on either personal merit or prior consent. Marriage, however, is a sign of the covenant and the election of God that forms the paradigm for family. There is a sense in which the original filial unit is programmed to "self-destruct" in terms of the priority of demands based on consanguinity when a new, con-

---

5. G. Ernest Wright, *The Biblical Doctrine of Man in Society* (London: SCM Press, 1954), pp. 18-19. Cited by C. Norman Kraus, *The Authentic Witness* (Grand Rapids: Eerdmans, 1979), p. 80.

6. Kraus, *Authentic Witness*, p. 79.

7. Hendrika Vande Kemp and G. Peter Schreck, "The Church's Ministry to Singles: A Family Model," *Journal of Religion and Health* 20 (1981): 141-55. My own analysis of the point this article attempts to make concerning consanguinity as now experienced through the church as the family of God is basically positive, though I must express caution at two points. First, there is a tendency to blur consanguinity and consensuality through a "spiritualizing" of the Old Testament covenant. This may be more of an ambiguity in the exposition than a fundamental problem. Second, it appears to me that a theological anthropology would place the emphasis neither upon relatedness nor on individual choosing, but rather upon that which uniquely determines our humanity — namely, coexistence in community. Through Jesus Christ, who became human in order to bring humanity into the "consanguinity" that exists between Father and Son through the Holy Spirit, a true order of human community exists that qualifies both married and single status. I do not see that including single persons in existing family-unit experiences as a form of "extended family" is the best way to accomplish this new family relationship.

sensual relation is established. Perhaps "self-destruct" is too vivid a metaphor. However, referring to the Old Testament language, "leaving" in order to effect a "cleaving" is a powerful and radical breaking up of one structure of relations to form a new one. Yet this "giving way" to a new order of relation is itself part of the creative and positive tension we referred to earlier. It is not a destructive and negative movement; rather, it is what parenting love has intended all along, if it has been truly grounded in the purpose of creating a capacity to form new covenant partnerships. Thus, suggests Norman Kraus, from the beginning, even as at the end, "the human family (community) living under God's covenant of peace (*shalom*) is the goal of creation."[8]

Returning now to our task of giving positive content to the concept of the church as the new family of God, we will set forth three aspects of the church as family. These aspects will relate to the developmental model of personal and spiritual formation that we presented earlier. The church, as the family of God, sets forth a new criterion of worth, a new form of parity, and a new context of belonging for each person in the kingdom of God.

Why *a new criterion of worth?* Does not one's existence in family give sufficient self-worth to each other? Yes — and No. As the foundation for family love, covenant love is not based on merit but on belonging. It was not because Israel was greater in number than other nations or had greater merit when compared to others that God chose and loved her. But, we are told, the Lord set his love upon Israel and chose her to be his own people "because the Lord loves you" (Deut. 7:7). Covenant love creates worth and is itself the criterion of worth. It is not erratic or idiosyncratic, but comes to expression as a bonding of God to his people, and of them to each other and to him through the social, religious, and political structure of their life as a people. The Israelites grew up in this social context knowing first of all that each belonged to this structure, and that each person's identity is grounded in this belonging.

It is the responsibility of parenting to reinforce this self-worth, ordinarily in a context where consanguinity is the fundamental criterion for acceptance. Infants ordinarily experience the "flesh and blood" or "kinship" ties first. To be told that one is the "spit an' image" of one's parent is a source of pride and self-worth for a youngster. Interestingly, this phrase is a contraction of "spirit and image," suggesting that flesh and blood relation also conveys the very formation of one's spirit in the likeness of another. In other words, this original kinship relation with one's family of origin entails an obligation not based on merit alone. As Robert Frost said, "Home is a place where, when you have to go there, they have to take you in"

However, the self-worth originally formed around the reality and security

---

8. Kraus, *Authentic Witness*, p. 81.

of belonging, no matter what, must be shifted to consensual relations, where the criterion for assessing self-worth is more functional than natural or biological. Failure to make this shift results in a failure of new relationships to support our identity. The stereotype of a disillusioned bride "going home to mother" as a result of a marital quarrel reflects this failure to make a critical adjustment in self-worth. On the other hand, it is also common for a woman to discover that her husband's criterion for self-worth has not completely shifted away from dependence upon his mother in critical times of need.

The church as the new family of God, however, is not formed by mere consensuality between its members. Through spiritual rebirth, we each become a brother or sister of Jesus Christ through adoption into the family of God. Consequently, we are brother or sister to each other. This new criterion of worth has a transcendent source and thus a permanent status. Husbands and wives are first of all brother and sister in Jesus Christ before they are husband and wife. Sons and daughters are also brother or sister to their father and mother before they are sons and daughters. This precedence, of course, is logical, not always chronological. Nevertheless, because it is theological, it does constitute a real precedence in each relationship. Unlike the human consanguinity that "self-destructs," this new consanguine relation, which is constituted by divine election in Jesus Christ, builds self-worth on that which will abide in and through life's changes as well as life's losses.

Each member of the Body of Christ receives the Spirit of Christ and is given a new standing with God in Christ. This does not happen merely "individualistically" or "privately," but corporately and publicly. Baptism is a community event as well as a personal and individual one. Yet the church as community does not become surrogate parents for young people nor does it replace the family as a social and domestic unit. In extreme cases it may appear to do so, but this is not its calling; thus, if indeed it must do so, it must also prepare for that function to "self-destruct." Individual members of family units as well as those who, for one reason or another, are "orphans" become peers in the Body of Christ as brother or sister. When this criterion for self-worth has become internalized prior to any critical point of change in family status, the individual can experience the transition with minimal trauma. "For my mother and father have forsaken me," says the Psalmist, "but the Lord will take me up" (Ps. 27:10). Yahweh asks, "Can a woman forget her sucking child, that she should have no compassion on the son of her womb?" and then answers, "Even these may forget, yet I will not forget you" (Isa. 49:15). The Hebrew child grew up with a criterion for self-worth that was not yet revealed to those outside the covenant. Thus, in all of our parenting there must also be weaning. Even the extended family, where grandfather and great-grandmother are part of the household, can become a sentimental attachment that provides no permanence in the midst of change. Brother and sister may be the only names we will need in heaven.

Here on earth, we have many names, and we wear many faces. Having been baptized into the new family of God, we are adopted into the filial relation that exists between God the Son and God the Father. We are brother and sister to God in Christ. And when we call each other brother and sister, this is more than an affected characteristic of a certain Christian life-style — it is a new criterion of our worth, and one that will survive.

In the new family of God, as brothers and sisters of Christ and therefore of one another, we also discover *a new form of parity*.[9] As we use it here, parity ought not to be confused with equality. By *parity* we mean equivalence of share rather than equality of role in a relation. In other words, parity means having full equivalence of partnership and value without having to have the same functional roles. Marriage relationships are meant to express parity between husband and wife, who share equally in the benefits of marriage (we hope), even though their respective roles may differ. Children equally are "family," with parents, though they are to obey their parents and parents are to instruct and discipline their children. In these cases, parity is related to equal status despite differing roles and responsibilities. Thus, parity is grounded in the commonality, or *koinonia*, that characterizes the life of the family.

However, not all social relationships are included in marriage and family life. The single adult who has left the parental home will find no ontological basis for parity in social contracts alone. In other words, social contracts will not provide a bonded relation in which the personal being of one is sustained and affirmed by the other(s). Parity in the sense that we mean it is a determinative of covenant love, not of contractual and performance-oriented social relations. An employer/employee relationship, for example, has no essential parity in terms of life-enhancing and person-reinforcing benefits. It is not that such contractual relationships cannot also express some dimension of parity, but parity is not the essential purpose of the relation between employer and employee as expressed in organizational line relationships, financial remuneration, or share in the company's profits.

The church as the new family of God, however, does offer a new form of parity — or at least it ought to. Not every member of the body has the same function and not always the same honor, says Paul. But there is still absolute parity: "If one member suffers, all suffer together; if one member is honored, all rejoice together" (1 Cor. 12:26). As Schreck and Vande Kemp have pointed out, the church often fails precisely at this point because it tends to segregate

---

9. For the concept of parity, I am indebted to Vande Kemp and Schreck, "The Church's Ministry."

members on the basis of married and single persons. A "ministry to singles" within the church, the authors stress, is no more valid that a separate ministry to racial or socioeconomic segments of the church family.[10] Without debating the merits of that assessment at this point, one might well agree with the basic premise behind the critique. The church's unique gift is its inclusive and transcending order of family life, which gives each member full parity in the *koinonia*.

Can the church promote stable marriages and healthy family life in society without abandoning the nonmarried and relegating them to the status of second-class citizens? It not only can, it must. And it will, if it teaches and practices a proper theology of family. It will be difficult, to be sure. The church family carries with it the strengths and weaknesses of the society in which it exists. It will be all too easy to assume that family life as the *koinonia* of the Body of Christ is identical with the social life of its members. It is not. The true *koinonia* of Christ is not only intergenerational but intramural as well. Not only are all parts of the body to function but they are to function together. If it should happen that momentarily — and even frequently — members of the Body of Christ forget that they are single or married, parents or children, and rejoice and suffer together as brothers and sisters, this will not damage or destroy homes and families! Instead, such experiences of parity liberate the organizational, administrative, and social role functions from having to carry the entire weight of personal worth.

One of the most controversial and confusing tendencies in our modern society is the pressure to force all basic relationships, both domestic and social, into the arena of competition for equality. The political pressure for passage of the Equal Rights Amendment is a case in point. Quite simple in its formulation, the amendment says, "Equality of rights under the law shall not be denied or abridged by the United States or by any State on account of sex." Opponents of the amendment fear that there are hidden assumptions in the language of the proposed law, which would undercut traditional and foundational structures of family life. If one of the hidden assumptions is that parity at the personal level is not possible until equality of role and function is achieved at the social level, then there could well be reason for concern. On the other hand, a long history and existing practices of unfair discrimination against women in the business world and marketplace seem to call for legal redress.

Nor is the church itself free from such confrontative and controversial issues regarding full parity for women with men in roles of leadership and ministry. Here, too, a long history of suppression of women at the social level

---

10. Ibid.

has formed a tradition within the church to which biblical texts can be attached in support of role discrimination as a command of God. Much wisdom and patience will be required, in our judgment, to separate the issue of parity from equality on the one hand and the natural order from the "supranatural" order on the other hand. When parity becomes confused with equality and the natural order confused with the supranatural order, the paradigm of covenant community disappears from view. In its place appears ideological and individualistic authority, which eventually betrays the goal of love as community.

Within the New Testament the mandate for parity within existing social and domestic structures and role relationships is a judgment against the power of the old orders, but, at the same time, it is a power to experience the full measure of belonging and grace that belongs to each one in the kingdom of God. Thus the apostle Paul can urge parents and children to live within constraints, slaves and masters to make their relationship work for the highest good, and husbands and wives to find liberation from practical role requirements through mutual submission and full partnership in the benefits of love and life (see Eph. 5-6). Quite clearly, the essential parity that exists as the very structure of the church as the new family of God seeks to overcome and transform all roles and relationships that belong to the old order, which is passing away. This, of course, creates a new form of social and domestic life that must be practiced before it can be credibly taught. And this leads us to consider a third aspect of the church as the family of God.

Before we do, however, we should summarize the first two aspects of the church as the new family of God. First, in this family of God persons have a new criterion of worth. Second, these persons have a new form of parity. These dimensions of personal existence are new because the church as the family of God becomes the contextualization of the eschatological reality where all temporal orders are relativized and fulfilled in the new humanity, wherein all who belong to God live in fellowship with him and with one another. There is a sense in which one might say that in the church this eschatological reality has already begun to dissolve the "form of this world" with its orders of creation and with the disorder of sin and disobedience. Without destroying the present order prematurely, nonetheless, the church as the family of God is the beginning of the transformation of these orders. In this new community, a new order of belonging is established in which Christ's order prevails — "I do not call you servants . . . but I call you friends" (John 15:15). Christ himself is the middle term in this coming together as friends.

We might say, therefore, that there is a third aspect of the church as the new family of God: *a new context of belonging* as members of God's family. This may be one way of understanding the somewhat quaint New Testament expression "household of faith." In his letter to the Galatian church Paul urges the believers to "do good to all men, and especially to those who are of the household of faith" (Gal. 6:10). *Household* is a much broader term than what we ordinarily mean by a nuclear family unit. It includes not only parents and children but other relatives who live with them, as well as servants or even slaves. The household is a microcosm of society itself, and provides a certain self-sufficiency as well as mutual interdependence to all who belong to it. Thus salvation is experienced not only by individuals; it "comes to a household" (Acts 16:31; John 4:53; cf. Gen. 7:1). The "household," in this sense, is the contextualization of one's personal life. It is in this context that worth and parity become real.

It is noteworthy that the renewal movement in the Roman Catholic Church following Vatican II strongly emphasized the domestic aspect of the church. Pope John Paul I, addressing a group of bishops from the United States in one of his few public speeches before his death, said that "the Christian family is so important, and its role so basic in transforming the world and in building up the kingdom of God, that the Council called it a 'domestic church.' "[11]

Commenting on this, David Thomas writes,

> We are invited to make present the love of God in human form. This takes place *in* the relationships in the family and *in* the relationships of the family to outsiders. These can all be sacramental relationships.... These are charisms, extraordinary gifts given by God, that qualify the recipients as ministers of the Lord, true disciples of the living Lord who remains alive especially through their many expressions of generosity, care, and service.[12]

The willingness of a Roman Catholic theologian not only to think of the church as a domestic unit (family) but to suggest that the relationships that take place in the domestic life of the church are of a sacramental nature reveals to us how seriously some are beginning to identify church with family.

What does this mean for us? Will this become another church program that promotes marriage as the cure for the loneliness and alienation of the unmarried adult? Or will the church as the family of God contextualize both the married and the unmarried, both the parents and the children, in the form of a "household of faith"? We hope the latter will be the case. But how is this possible in the contemporary social order where household means, in IRS language, the smallest sociological unit with a single wage earner at the head? It would be desperate enough if we were to consider the more typical nuclear family unit a household, but "parents without partners" also constitute a sizable

---

11. *Lumen Gentium* II, cited by David M. Thomas in *Family Life and the Church* (New York: Paulist Press, 1979), p. 2.

12. Ibid., pp. 36-37.

number of households under this definition. "One of the problems of family life in contemporary society," writes Thomas, "is the isolation felt by the individual nuclear family."[13] Rather than view this as the ideal of the domestic life of the church, he suggests that the church will need to reconstitute family through the facilitating of a "domestic church" as a basic cell of the larger ecclesiastical unit. These cells, or "block units," will begin to function like "households of faith." They will perform many functions, including some aspects of education, stabilization of economic existence for members of the group, prayer and liturgy, and even the evangelization of the larger community in which they exist.[14]

These are not new concepts, of course; various sectors of the Christian church have attempted on an experimental basis to create new forms and models of the church through the cell-group process. It would probably be a mistake, however, to substitute the concept of a small group for that of family, and it most certainly would be a mistake to break down the precarious structure of family life as it presently exists in the nuclear family unit. Thus, the question we are asking is this: To what family, as a domestic unit (or household of faith), does the nuclear family belong? In one sense, each adult who no longer lives with an original family unit has experienced a "broken household." We tend to think of children whose parents have divorced, and of the divorced parents themselves, as coming from "broken homes." But this is only half the truth. The man or woman who leaves a parental home to set up his or her own home, whether with a marriage partner, a roommate, or alone, has experienced a "broken household." The original filial unit is designed for self-destruction when children "leave home" and strike out on their own. It is easy (relatively speaking) to set up housekeeping by renting a room or an apartment, and easier still to create a new home through marriage (even at $20.00, the cost of a marriage license is the smallest obstacle to the setting up of housekeeping). But even a so-called Christian marriage is not yet a "household of faith." And how much less than a "household of faith" is a room with a single person, or even one shared with a roommate?

As we have said, marriage is not meant to be the sanctification of the human disorder of solitary existence. Rather, it needs to be sanctified itself by belonging to a "household of faith." Far too many "family units," as a statistic on the latest census reports, are actually islands of quiet despair in the sea of humanity. And this is often at their best! More often, life in these families is demeaning and destructive to human personhood itself. No, it is the household

---

13. Ibid., p. 109.
14. Ibid., pp. 108-9.

of faith which is the sanctification of marriage and family, as well as of the unmarried and nonfamily persons.

For the ancient Israelite, the covenant community constituted the "household of faith," and consequently also sanctified families and individuals. Even as the covenant community had its origin in the tribe, and the tribe in the "household" of Jacob, so the household of Jacob has its consummation and ultimate meaning in the covenant community. The breaking up of one family unit in order to form another did not constitute the breaking down of the "household of faith." The covenant community contextualized both individual persons and family units in the eschatological reality of being "people of God." In this context, the worth and parity of each person was assured, despite the injustice and tyranny of the old order.

I will rephrase the question: To what family, or household of faith, does the family belong without losing its character as a domestic community where ordinary and daily life is affirmed and supported? Does it belong to the church as the family of God? Doesn't this mean, then, that the church itself must become the "household of faith?" And if so, won't this mean that the church becomes both the sanctification and celebration of that commonality (*koinonia*) that exists between people who are the "friends" of Jesus and who exist for and with each other? Shouldn't these "households of faith," by whatever definition or form they take, be the center of the liturgical life of the people of God, even as they are the source of nourishment and support for the daily and ordinary life of the members? Shouldn't Christian baptism be baptism into a "household of faith," where one is immediately joined with other "brothers and sisters," and shouldn't the eucharist be celebrated by and with those who have a stake in each other's "daily bread?" Until this takes place, how can the church be the true people of God? And how can renewal of the family take place without the renewal of the "household of faith" itself?

We cannot rightly pray "forgive us our trespasses" and "give us this day our daily bread" until we have prayed "thy kingdom come, . . . on earth as it is in heaven." And when I pray this prayer, I surrender my right and privilege as husband or father, and I ask for and positively seek the right and privileges of my brothers and sisters to sit at table with me and so make visible the kingdom of God. Here there is no room for a separate ministry to "singles," for they are my "household of faith" — we are each from broken homes, and in need of a household where there is healing.

We began this chapter with the question, "In light of Jesus' teaching concerning the new order that exists in the kingdom of God, can the Christian church today make family life a means of spiritual formation, and the building of the family its central task?" We can now answer No, not its central task. The central task of the church is to be a reconciled and reconciling community.

However, in being and doing this, the church grasps whatever is broken and brings it toward wholeness. It touches whatever is orphaned and creates family. It saves families by saving husbands and wives from destroying each other through impossible ultimatums. It saves parents from having to determine their children's destinies, and it saves children from having to enshrine their parents in their own goals in order to carry them with them. Jesus calls each to be his brother and sister and so makes brothers and sisters out of all who come to him. God is family.

And brothers and sisters we shall all be, there.

CHAPTER TWELVE

WHAT KIND OF FAMILY
IS THE CHURCH?

T HE chapter title above betrays my bias. As I see it, the church is a family, or perhaps a family of families. How we perceive the idea of family will determine in subtle ways how we perceive the church.[1]

Admittedly, the notion of the church as a family of families is only a metaphor in the same way the church is referred to in Scripture as a body, a temple, and so forth. Perhaps in terms of the present discussion the concept of household would be the closest scriptural equivalent available. If we say that the church is the household of faith, what are we really saying?

In order to answer this question from the point of view of the social sciences, what I would like to do is contrast three terms from the fields of sociology and anthropology and then conclude with a fourth alternative that preserves what I suggest to be the genius of the New Testament metaphor of the church as the household of God.

As we have stated throughout this book, to begin a theology of the family with the idea of marriage at its core is to miss significantly a key element in understanding the family as God has created it. We have chosen instead to begin with the dual notions of parenting and covenant. The former has to do with the organizational core of our social theology and the latter has to do with the affective core, that is, that which holds the family as an organization together.

THE CONJUGAL NATURE
OF THE FAMILY

Lest I appear to be obscurantist, I must point out that there is a reason that our culture has come to the place where it emphasizes the conjugal or marital

---

1. See Dennis Guernsey, *A New Design for Family Ministry* (Elgin, IL: David C. Cook, 1983).

system. William Goode writes that the sense of the nuclear family or the conjugal system is a "theoretical construction derived from intuition and observation in which several crucial variables have been combined to form a hypothetical structural harmony."[2] The reason the conjugal family comes into particular importance is that in an industrial and technological society that requires mobility and a fluid population to support the society, the marriage relationship tends to come to the fore.

Therefore, an industrial economy requires a conjugal emphasis rather than an emphasis on extended kin. Placing the greater importance upon a marriage becomes the ideal — one that the society and the culture must support in order to function. Relevant to our discussion would be the question of whether or not the church has adopted the motif of the broader culture.

Schreck and Vande Kemp identify a major conceptual weakness in the approach most Christian literature takes regarding the family.[3] They contend that the church's conjugal focus, that is, its focus on marriage as the core of its family ministry, systematically excludes those who are not married, giving them a sense of alienation at worst and a sense of not belonging at best. They conclude that a theology of the family that is marriage centered reflects a culture that is marriage centered, however necessary that emphasis might be.

The result of this emphasis in the broader culture is a single versus married mentality that produces a lack of community except between those of a similar kind. Further, it often produces in the single person an openness to life-styles that are itinerant, casual, and temporary.

In the church the result is to push the single to the fringe, to a distinct position of not belonging. Schreck and Vande Kemp appeal to the church to redefine its implicit definition of what a family is and to shape its ministry accordingly.

The contemporary panic in the church over the issue of divorce has yielded ancillary results beyond the need to emphasize the sanctity of marriage. Do we really intend to relegate those who are not married to a status of second-class citizens? How do we square such a result with the scriptural teaching regarding celibacy? What of the teaching about widows?

Whatever the emphasis in the broader culture, clearly there is strong teaching in the New Testament that precludes an emphasis in which only those who are married are first-class citizens and all of the rest second-class.

---

2. W. J. Goode, *World Revolution and Family Patterns* (New York: The Free Press, 1963), p. 7.

3. Hendrika Vande Kemp and G. Peter Schreck, "The Church's Ministry to Singles: A Family Model," *Journal of Religion and Health* 20 (1981): 141-55.

Therefore, we must conclude that a theology of the family that centers upon the conjugal nature of the family is inadequate.

THE CONSANGUINE NATURE OF THE FAMILY

Ralph Turner defines consanguine as a principle in kinship organization.[4] He quotes Ralph Linton, who identifies the major issue at stake if the family is defined as consanguine at its core. According to Linton,

> A society may capitalize the sexual attraction between adults and do all it can to give permanence to mated relationships or a society may capitalize the associations formed on an asexual basis during childhood reinforcing them and continuing them into adult life. Such asexual associations are most readily established between individuals brought up in the same functional family unit, that is real or socially designated brothers and sisters. In other words, the association of adults which is the necessary nucleus of any family as a functional unit may be based upon either conjugal or consanguine relationships. In societies organized upon the conjugal basis we picture the authentic functional family as consisting of a nucleus of spouses and their offspring surrounded by a fringe of relatives.... In those organized on a consanguine basis we can picture the authentic family as the nucleus of blood relatives surrounded by a fringe of spouses.[5]

The term *consanguine* focuses upon relationships that are tied together by blood or geneology. In many cultures ties are maintained based upon the blood relationship of the family members and nothing more. Although this kind of relationship dominates much of the world, especially in the underdeveloped countries, a theology that is based upon geneology or blood ties would tend to relegate the church to an agency designed to perpetuate privilege and status, as was the case in the medieval church in which membership was determined on the basis of one's familial ties.

Jesus' teaching about the "new birth" mediates against just such a consanguine focus. A person's first birth is not enough. There must be a second birth based upon one's relationship with God apart from one's relationship with any earthly family.

Thus, an evangelical theology cannot accept a theology of the family that is consanguine in its focus and emphasis.

---

4. R. Turner, *Family Interaction* (New York: John Wiley and Sons, 1970).
5. Ralph Linton, *The Study of Man* (New York: Appleton-Century-Crofts, 1936), p. 159.

THE CONSENSUAL NATURE
OF THE CHURCH

Schreck and Vande Kemp argue for a third emphasis for the church, based upon the voluntary associations that exist in the church. They refer to this emphasis as "consensual." In the sociological literature, relationships that are based solely upon choice are said to come under the category of voluntary associations. In no case do such relationships fall under the category of family. In fact, they are considered to be mutually exclusive.

Such is the deficiency of a consensual focus for the church. It ultimately defines the church as a system of individuals whose relationships with one another are based upon the choices and associations they make rather than on their family ties, however those ties may be defined. Again, we cannot accept this view of the nature of the church.

THE COLLATERAL NATURE
OF THE FAMILY

In Chapter Eleven we read the following statement:

> The church as the new family of God, however, is not formed by mere consensuality between its members. Through spiritual rebirth, we each become a brother or sister of Jesus Christ through adoption into the family of God. Consequently, we are brother or sister to each other. This new criterion of worth has a transcendent source and thus a permanent status. Husbands and wives are first of all brother and sister in Jesus Christ before they are husband and wife. Sons and daughters are also brother or sister to their father and mother before they are sons and daughters. . . . Unlike the human consanguinity that "self-destructs," this new consanguine relation, which is constituted by divine election in Jesus Christ, builds self-worth on that which will abide in and through life's changes as well as life's losses.

But is this new relationship between brother and sister really consanguine — or should we use another term? Ralph Turner speaks of "collateral relations" between brother and sister. According to Turner,

> It was the discovery of the continuing importance of sibling and even cousin relationships that posed a challenge for our most recent forms of traditional family sociological theory. The picture of a secular society in which each person sought out friends and associations on the basis of common interest or reciprocal usefulness while rejecting all but the most insistent ties based upon tradition must surely be modified to accommodate the primary importance of siblings and their families and even cousins in voluntary social life.[6]

---

6. Turner, *Family Interaction*, p. 442.

Consistently, collateral relations are the most permanent, on-going relationships between human persons. On the whole they outlast marital, filial, and even friendship relationships.

Why is this so? As an explanation, in his discussion of the contrast between friendship and collateral relationships, Turner notes that one can be friends with his or her siblings,

> but there is something different about being friends just because you are brothers or cousins which provides a little more defense against these difficulties than do some of the avenues of achieved friendship. There is something relaxing about a relationship in which you can never be much more than you really are because the others know too much about you and about your past to forget it entirely.[7]

Following Turner's line of thought, I would like to coin a term: *siblial*. A "sib" by definition is a "group of persons unilaterally descended from a real or supposed ancestor." A sibling is a person in a sib relationship on the level of a brother or sister. I would suggest that the problem with consanguine relationships is that the tendency is to focus upon the parental/filial relationship. The problem with conjugal relationships is that the emphasis is upon the husband/wife relationship. Siblial relationships, however, are those in which people are committed to one another and see each other and accept each other as brothers and sisters. We are "joint-heirs" with Jesus Christ.

According to this model both parental/filial and conjugal/consensual relationships are important. But there comes a maturing of relationships in which we belong to each other and are responsible for one another. We are family, but the nature of family now becomes collateral/siblial. In that mystery of brother and sister there is a sense of commitment in a growing bond that pulls us to one another. The continuing functions of family and the necessary importance of the family as a unit can be very much served by a commitment that is siblial.

When the New Testament writers use siblial terms they were not meant to be mere euphemisms. "Brother" and "sister" are not simply pious jargon. They are real, permanent, and predictive. The church is in fact a family of families and the dynamic of that familial organization is our relationship with our Lord who then calls us to be brother and sister to one another. Because of him we are "sibs."

---

7. Ibid., p. 443.

Bibliography

Abramson, P., H. R. Cutler, and R. W. Kantz. "Social Power and Commitment." *American Sociological Review* 23 (Feb. 1958): 15-22.

Adams, Jay. *Competent to Counsel.* Nutley, NJ: Presbyterian and Reformed, 1972.

Anderson, Ray S. *On Being Human.* Grand Rapids: Eerdmans, 1982.

Balswick, Jack. "The Psychological Captivity of Evangelicalism." Fuller Theological Seminary, n.d.

Bandura, A., and R. H. Walters. *Social Learning and Personality Development.* New York: Holt, Rinehart and Winston, 1963.

Barth, Karl. *Church Dogmatics* III/1. Edited by G. W. Bromiley and T. F. Torrance. Edinburgh: T. & T. Clark, 1969.

Baum, Gregory. *Religion and Alienation.* New York: Paulist Press, 1975.

Baumrind, Diana. "Current Patterns of Parental Authority." Developmental Psychology Monograph Series, vol. 4, no. 1, pt. 2.

Becker, Ernest. *The Denial of Death.* New York: Macmillan, The Free Press, 1973.

Becker, H. S. "Notes on the Concept of Commitment." *American Journal of Sociology* 66 (July 1960): 32-40.

Behm, J. "Nouthesia." In *The Theological Dictionary of the New Testament.* Edited by Gerhard Kittel and Gerhard Friedrich, 4:1019. Grand Rapids: Eerdmans, 1967.

Bender, Ross. *Christians in Families.* Scottdale, PA: Herald Press, 1982.

Berger, Brigitte, and Peter Berger. *The War Over the Family.* Garden City, NY: Doubleday, Anchor Press, 1983.

Bertram, G. "Paideia." In *The Theological Dictionary of the New Testament.* Edited by Gerhard Kittel and Gerhard Friedrich, 5:596-625. Grand Rapids: Eerdmans, 1967.

Bettelheim, B. *Dialogues with Mothers.* Glencoe: The Free Press, 1962.

Bilezikian, Gilbert. *Beyond Sex Roles: A Guide for the Study of Female Roles in the Bible.* Grand Rapids: Baker Book House, 1985.

Bonhoeffer, Dietrich. *The Cost of Discipleship.* London: SCM Press, 1959.

————. *Ethics.* New York: Macmillan, 1965.

Boulding, K. E. "General Systems Theory — The Skeleton of Science." In *General Systems* 1 (1956): 11-17. Edited by L. von Bertalanffy. Reprinted from *Management Science* 2 (1956): 197-208.

Bowen, Murray. *Family Therapy in Clinical Practice.* New York: Aronson, 1978.

Bowlby, John. *Attachment*. New York: Basic Books, 1969.

Brim, Orville, and Stanton Wheeler. *Socialization after Childhood*. New York: John Wiley and Sons, 1966.

Brody, W. M. "A Cybernetic Approach to Family Therapy." In *Family Therapy and Disturbed Families*. Edited by G. H. Zeek and I. Boszormenyi-Nagi. Palo Alto, CA: Science and Behavior Books, 1967.

Bromiley, Geoffrey. *God and Marriage*. Grand Rapids: Eerdmans, 1980.

Bronfenbrenner, Urie. *The Ecology of Human Development*. Cambridge: Harvard University Press, 1979.

Brown, Colin, ed. "Separate, Divide." In *The New International Dictionary of New Testament Theology*. 3:534-43. Grand Rapids: Zondervan; Exeter: Paternoster Press, 1978.

Brunner, Emil. *Love and Marriage*. London: Collins, The Fontana Library, 1970.

Buber, Martin. *Between Man and Man*. London: Collins, The Fontana Library, 1963.

Buckley, W. *Sociology and Modern Systems Theory*. Englewood Cliffs, NJ: Prentice-Hall, 1967.

————, ed. *Modern Systems Research for the Behavioral Scientist*. Chicago: Aldine, 1968.

Cahill, Lisa Sowle. *Between the Sexes: Foundations for a Christian Ethics of Sexuality*. Philadelphia: Fortress Press, 1985.

Cannon, W. B. *The Wisdom of the Body*. New York: W. Norton and Company, 1939.

Capra, Fritjof. *The Turning Point*. New York: Bantam Books, 1983.

Clark, Stephen. *Man and Woman in Christ*. Ann Arbor: Servant Books, 1980.

Dana, H. E., and J. R. Mantey. *A Manual Grammar of the Greek New Testament*. New York: Macmillan, 1927.

Dean, D. G., and C. P. Spanier. "Commitment: an Overlooked Variable in Marital Adjustment." *Sociological Focus* 7 (1974): 113-18.

DeLamater, J. *The Study of Political Commitment*. Washington, D.C.: American Sociological Association, 1973.

Dobson, James. *Dare to Discipline*. Glendale, CA: Regal Books, 1974.

Dreikurs, Rudolf. *Children: The Challenge*. New York: Hawthorne Books, 1964.

Eddington, Sir Arthur. *The Nature of the Physical World*. Ann Arbor: University of Michigan Press, 1958.

Erikson, Erik. *Childhood and Society*. New York: Norton and Company, 1960.

Eshleman, J. R., and J. N. Clarke. *Intimacy, Commitments and Marriage: Development of Relationships*. Boston: Allyn and Bacon, 1978.

Fraiberg, Selma. *The Magic Years*. New York: Charles Scribner, 1968.

Framo, J. S. *Family Interaction*. New York: Springer, 1972.

Freud, Anna. "Remarks in a Panel Discussion." *International Journal of Psycho-Analysis* 49:506-7.

Gecos, Viktor. "Parental Behavior and Dimensions of Adolescent Self-Evaluation." *Sociometry* 34 (Dec.): 466-82.

Gill, Robin. "From Sociology to Theology." In *Sociology and Theology*. Edited by David Martin, John Orme Mills, and W. S. F. Pickering. New York: St. Martin's Press, 1980.

Goode, W. J. *World Revolution and Family Patterns*. New York: The Free Press, 1963.

Guernsey, Dennis B. *A New Design for Family Ministry*. Elgin, IL: David C. Cook, 1983.

Haley, J. *Techniques of Family Therapy*. New York: Basic Books, 1967.

Hall, A. D., and R. E. Fagen. "Definition of a System." *General Systems* 1 (1956): 18-28.

Harlow, H. F., et al. "Learning to Love." *The American Scientist* 54, no. 3 (1966): 244-72.

Hobart, C. W. "Commitment, Value Conflict, and the Future of the American Family." *Journal of Marriage and Family* (Nov. 1960): 405-12.

Hodge, Charles. *Systematic Theology*. Vol. 3. New York: Scribner and Company; London and Edinburgh: T. Nelson and Sons, 1891.

Horner, Althea. *Object Relations and the Developing Ego in Therapy*. New York: Jason Aronson, 1979.

Johnson, M. P. "Commitment: A Conceptual Structure and Empirical Application." *Sociological Quarterly* 14 (1973): 395-406.

_____. "Personal and Structural Commitment: Sources of Consistency in the Development of Relationships." Department of Sociology, The Pennsylvania State University, 1978.

Johnson, R. A., F. Kast, and J. Rosenzweig. *The Theory and Management of Systems*. New York: McGraw-Hill, 1967.

Jones, E., and H. B. Girard. *Foundations of Social Psychology*. New York: John Wiley and Sons, 1967.

Kiesler, C. A. *The Psychology of Commitment*. New York: Academic Press, 1971.

Klimek, David. *Beneath Mate Selection and Marriage*. New York: Van Nostrand Reinhold, 1979.

Knight, George A. F. *I AM: This is My Name*. Grand Rapids: Eerdmans, 1983.

Kraus, C. Norman. *The Authentic Witness*. Grand Rapids: Eerdmans, 1979.

Lamb, Michael. *The Role of the Father in Child Development*. New York: John Wiley and Sons, 1976.

Lasch, Christopher. *Haven in a Heartless World*. New York: Basic Books, 1977.

Linton, Ralph. *The Study of Man*. New York: Appleton-Century-Crofts, 1936.

Luther, Martin. *The Works of Martin Luther*. Edited by Henry Eyster Jacobs. Vol. 5. Philadelphia: Muhlenberg Press, 1915–43.

Lynn, David. *The Father: His Role in Child Development*. Monterey, CA: Brooks/Cole, 1975.

Maccoby, E., and C. Jacklin. *The Psychology of Sex Differences*. Stanford: Stanford University Press, 1974.

McLean, Stuart D. *Humanity in the Thought of Karl Barth*. Edinburgh: T. & T. Clark, 1981.

Macmurray, John. *Reason and Emotion*. London: Faber and Faber, 1935.

—————. *Persons in Relation*. London: Faber and Faber, 1961.

Manson, T. W. *The Teaching of Jesus*. 2nd ed. Cambridge: Cambridge University Press, 1935.

Maslow, A. H. "A Theory of Human Motivation." *Psychological Review* 50 (1943): 370-96.

Mayo, Clara. "Man: Not Only an Individual, But a Member." *Zygon* 3 (March 1968).

Mead, G. H. *Mind, Self, and Society*. Chicago: University of Chicago Press, 1934.

Mead, Margaret. "Marriage in Two Steps." *Redbook*, July 1966, 48ff.

Mendenhall, G. E. "Covenant." In *The Interpreter's Dictionary of the Bible*. New York: Abingdon Press, 1962.

Miller, Arthur. *After the Fall*. Middlesex, England: Penguin Books, 1968.

Minuchin, Salvador. *Families and Family Therapy*. Cambridge, MA: Harvard University Press, 1974.

—————, et al. *Psychosomatic Families*. Cambridge, MA: Harvard University Press, 1978.

Murstein, Bernard I. *Love, Sex and Marriage Through the Ages*. New York: Springer, 1974.

Narramore, Bruce. *Help! I'm A Parent*. Grand Rapids: Zondervan, 1972.

Neill, John R., and David P. Kniskern, eds. *From Psyche to System: The Evolving Therapy of Carl Whitaker*. New York: The Guilford Press, 1982.

Niebuhr, H. Richard. *The Responsible Self*. New York: Harper and Row, 1963.

Ogburn, W. F. "The Changing Functions of the Family." *The Family* 19 (1938): 139-43.

Pannenberg, Wolfhart. *Anthropology in Theological Perspective*. Translated by Matthew J. O'Connell. Philadelphia: Westminster Press, 1985.

Parsons, Talcott. *Family Socialization and Interaction Process*. Glencoe: The Free Press, 1955.

Polanyi, Michael. *Personal Knowledge*. London: Routledge and Kegan Paul, 1958.

Rahner, Karl. "Ideas for a Theology of Childhood." In *Theological Investigations*. New York: Seabury Press, 1977.

Roszak, Theodore. *Person/Planet*. Garden City, NY: Doubleday, Anchor Press, 1979.

Russell, Letty. *The Future of Partnership*. Philadelphia: Westminster Press, 1979.

Saint Exupery, Antoine de. *The Little Prince*. New York: Harcourt, Brace and World, Harbrace Paperbound Library, 1943.

Sears, R. R. *Identification and Child Rearing*. Stanford: Stanford University Press, 1965.

—————, et al. *Patterns of Child Rearing*. New York: Row, Peterson, 1957.

Shaffer, Peter. *Equus*. New York: Avon Books, 1974.

Small, Dwight. *Christian: Celebrate Your Sexuality*. Old Tappan, NJ: Revell, 1974.

—————. *The Right to Remarry*. Old Tappan, NJ: Revell, 1975.

Speer, D. C. "Family Systems: Morphostasis and Morphogenesis, or 'Is Homeostasis Enough?'" *Family Process* 9 (1979): 259-78.

Spitz, R. A. "The Role of Ecological Factors in Emotional Development in Infancy." *Child Development* 20 (1949): 145-55.

Steiner, Ivan D. *Group Process and Productivity*. New York: Academic Press, 1972.

Straus, M. A. "Power and Support Structure of the Family in Relation to Socialization." *Journal of Marriage and Family* 26 (Aug.): 318-26.

Sullivan, H. S. *The Interpersonal Theory of Psychiatry*. New York: Norton, 1953.

Theodorson, G. A., and A. G. Theodorson. *A Modern Dictionary of Sociology*. New York: Thomas Y. Crowell, 1969.

Thibault, J., and H. H. Kelley. *The Social Psychology of Groups*. New York: John Wiley and Sons, 1959.

Thomas, David M. *Family Life and the Church*. New York: Paulist Press, 1979.

Thomas, D. L., and A. J. Weigert. "Socialization and Adolescent Conformity to Significant Others: A Cross-national Analysis." *American Sociological Review* 36 (Oct.): 835-47.

Torrance, Thomas F. *God and Rationality*. London: Oxford University Press, 1971.

_____. *Divine and Contingent Order*. Oxford: Oxford University Press, 1981.

Turner, R. *Family Interaction*. New York: John Wiley and Sons, 1970.

Vande Kemp, Hendrika, and G. P. Schreck. "The Church's Ministry to Singles: A Family Model." *Journal of Religion and Health* 20 (1981): 141-55.

von Balthasar, Hans Urs. *A Theological Anthropology*. New York: Sheed and Ward, 1967.

von Bertalanffy, L. "General Systems Theory — A Critical Review." *General Systems* 7 (1962): 1-20.

_____. *General Systems Theory*. New York: George Braziller, 1968.

Weigert, A. J., and D. L. Thomas. "Socialization and Religiousity: A Cross-national Analysis of Catholic Adolescents." *Sociometry* 33 (Sept.): 305-26.

Whitaker, Carl, and Augustus Napier. *The Family Crucible*. New York: Harper and Row, 1978.

Winnecott, Donald. *The Child, The Family, and the Outside World*. New York: Penguin Books, 1975.

Wright, G. Ernest. *The Biblical Doctrine of Man in Society*. London: SCM Press, 1954.

Wright, H. Norman. *Marriage Counseling*. San Francisco: Harper and Row, 1982.

Index